ROBERT JAMES MERRETT

Daniel Defoe's Moral and Rhetorical Ideas

© 1980 by Robert James Merrett

ELS Editions
Department of English
University of Victoria
Victoria, BC
Canada V8W 3W1
www.elseditions.com

Founding Editor: Samuel L. Macey

General Editor: Luke Carson

Printed by CreateSpace

No part of this publication may be reproduced, stored in a retrieval system or transmitted, in any form or by any means. Without the prior written consent of the publisher or a licence from The Canadian Copyright Licensing Agency (Access Copyright). For an Access Copyright licence, visit *www.accesscopyright.ca* or call toll free to 1-800-893-5777.

English literary studies monograph series
ISSN 0829-7681 ; 19
ISBN-10 0-920604-36-6
ISBN-13 978-0-920604-36-6

CONTENTS

	Preface	7
CHAPTER 1	Defoe and Religious Sense	9
CHAPTER 2	Natural and Divine Law	30
CHAPTER 3	The Revolution of 1688	48
CHAPTER 4	Language and Narrative	67
CHAPTER 5	The Uses of Narrative	88
	Notes	106

To my parents

PREFACE

Of so much Force is Ironical Righteousness, that the blackest Agents are fittest to be made the brightest Examples of it; since also the greatest and best Principles are often illustrated by their most infamous, and consequently, by their compleatist Contraries.[1]

Although this study is not concerned immediately with the curious and paradoxical didacticism of Defoe's major narratives, it does seek to provide, by demonstrating that he is a more deliberate thinker and a more calculatedly provocative teacher than is perhaps usually conceded, a context for the appreciation of the part which narrative contraries and dialectic play in his fiction. There is, of course, no denying that his writings give rise to critical dilemmas on account of authorial carelessness and that commentators have been troubled by the difficult relation of traditional and modern elements in his thought and by the problem of his conscious artistry. Since Defoe is not a systematic thinker and since he usually subordinates aesthetic to moral considerations, it remains a peculiar challenge to explain his use of ideas and of rhetorical strategies. Certainly, Professor Novak's studies, to which the present one is indebted, have gone a long way in establishing that Defoe 'kept abreast of all the new ideas of his day, but retained his faith in his conscience and the Bible.'[2] But there is still scope to examine Defoe's disposition of ideas in argument and narration, for there is not much agreement on this subject. For instance, whereas Professor Sutherland judges that Defoe generally takes an almost excessively logical interest in making religious arguments, Novak maintains that Defoe was much more likely to rely on rational as distinct from religious appeals to his contemporaries.[3] On the other hand, in his recent book Peter Earle stresses the unique aspects of Defoe's view of the world: he defends the conventional position that Defoe was a better entertainer than teacher on the unusual grounds that the writer reduced his observations of the world to a limited set of preconceived ideas. Earle thereby suggests that, in addition to being wrapped up in his own image of reality, Defoe was unprepared to reconcile his worldly and religious ideas in his writings.[4]

It is the contention of this study that Defoe exerted himself in the expression of his moral ideas and that he possessed a precise sense of his role as an exponent of these ideas. After detailing his subjection of philosophical to religious ideas as a means of defining his notion of moral sense and after explaining his rhetorical exploitation of arguments from natural law, the study moves on to describe the connections Defoe made between political, social, and religious issues. Next, it expounds Defoe's awareness of the qualities of language and narrative that provided him with resources for linking social and religious themes, and, finally, it presents evidence of his various deliberative applications of narrative to his recurring moral concerns.

Besides gratefully acknowledging the various influences of recent Defoe scholarship upon this study, I wish to profess the formative effect upon my thinking about Defoe of the late Professor T. J. B. Spencer of The Shakespeare Institute in The University of Birmingham.

CHAPTER 1

Defoe and Religious Sense

It is Religion alone, which is the Bond of Virtue in the World; the Awe of a Divine Power, and a Sense of the Majesty and Vengeance of Heaven, being alone able to restrain the Vices and Lusts of Men. It seems very natural then, that as a Sense of Religion dyes, the love of Virtue must also decay; and hence it is, that generally speaking, our Deists and Free-Thinkers are profane, and *Free-Actors* also; for,—erasing the Awe of God in their Hearts, they plead immediately, and of Course, for a Freedom in all Manner of Vice,—using the Pretence of Liberty for a Justification of Crime, as if the Liberty God gave to Man of being a free Agent, disengaged him entirely from all restraint of Laws, whether Human or Divine.[1]

Defoe's preoccupation with religious sense is manifest. An awareness of the divine and an appreciation of spiritual awe constitute for him the authority of moral knowledge and the source of moral behaviour. His dislike of the unorthodoxy of deism partly represents his unwillingness to consider morality independently of religion. In his view, deism was a way of thinking which inappropriately tried to free itself from religious sense. Hence, he regarded deists as necessarily immoral and irreligious. Without a religious sense individuals could but act, and rationalize their actions, irresponsibly, whereas those who respected religious sense naturally experienced a social bond. Clearly, Defoe valued religious sense as much for its cohesive, cultural force as for its indication of an individual's spiritual state.

Defoe's estimation of religious sense led him to depreciate systems of thought which ignored religion and revelation and, although he defended his position with precise philosophical arguments, the assumptions behind these arguments are irreducibly religious. In Defoe's mind, knowledge and science were incapable of absolute truth because of the fallibility of human perception: reason's discourse with natural phenomena and second causes could never attain the truth essential to morality. God was the single source of this truth so that only those who worshipped him as the first cause of creation could draw upon this source.[2] On the other hand, those who pretended to ignore fallibility added heresy to self-deception.

Men affecting to search into what is impossible they should clearly discover, learn to doubt, because they cannot describe, and deny the Existence because they cannot explain the Manner of what they inquire after; as if a thorow impossibility of their acting by their Sense upon Objects beyond its Reach was an Evidence against their Being.[3]

Obviously, Defoe did not believe that reality is simply the product of the individual mind, nor did he hold that empirical experience is the test of existence. In other words, he did not equate the order of being with the order of knowing. Yet neither did he deny progress to knowledge. Indeed, he often promoted natural science and celebrated the benefits to mankind of experimental philosophy. For instance, he praised Bacon, Boyle, and Newton for converting nature's secrets into human knowledge and for making the probing of nature's mysteries a permissible and respectable activity.[4] Nonetheless, Defoe felt compelled to preserve the integrity of religion against some of the harmful influences of science. To achieve this he treated religion as a superior and ultimate body of knowledge.

He was sure that both rational processes and logical demonstrations are inferior to religious knowledge and that faith should be understood only in biblical terms.

I must come back to the Scriptures, Every thing needful to our life here, and passage hence, or usefull to our being hereafter, is contain'd in them: And the Scripture says expressly, *This kind of Faith is not obtain'd but by prayer and fasting.*[5]

Since, for Defoe, the sacred mysteries of religion existed beyond the reach of rational formulation, the reason of syllogism, of mathematical proof, and of scientific hypothesis was not directly relevant to faith and spirit. He also regarded ontological and cosmological arguments for God's existence as irrelevant to religious sense. He argued that intellectual familiarization with the problems of God's existence merely achieved ideas of analogy, and he felt that these ideas could by no means substitute for a faithful relationship with God. Defoe disclaimed the relation of reason to faith partly because of the danger of psychological rationalization. Reason could give rise to intellectual distinctions and equations which are arbitrary and self-deceiving.

Men by nice Reasoning, may distinguish themselves into, and out of any Religion, or any Opinion; especially when they think to reconcile every part of their Religion to their Reason.[6]

Defoe realized that reason by itself cannot expound the integrity of religion. A survey of his reactions to various philosophers shows what resources he thought that he could draw on to defend religious sense as a special kind of knowledge.

Defoe considered Bacon a Christian philosopher.[7] Not only did he admire Bacon's programme for learning and his rescue of knowledge from scholasticism but also he appreciated Bacon's attitude towards nature because it did not seem to challenge God's authority. To Defoe, Bacon appeared to have reconciled the claims of religion and of knowledge. Defoe, like Bacon, was intolerant of complacent ignorance, as is evident when, in a passage promoting scientific advances, he cites Proverbs XVIII, 2: 'A Fool hath no delight in understanding, but that his heart may discover itself.' By this citation he indicates his belief that knowledge of nature is a religious obligation.[8] Although, as we have seen, Defoe refused to countenance human reasoning as a model for religious knowledge, he thought it legitimate that mathematical knowledge should excite the souls of men to discover nature's secrets. While, then, Defoe was not single-mindedly enthusiastic about a scientific model of knowledge, he still respected Bacon's scientific method: it seemed less presumptuous and more reverent than the methods of other philosophers, possibly because Bacon admitted that the grace of God helped man to learn about the works of creation.[9] Bacon, too, insisted that man impose restrictions upon his scientific inquiry rather than upon nature: man in his search for knowledge had always to bear his mortality in mind, had to apply his knowledge to contentment, and could never presume to comprehend divine mysteries.[10] Furthermore, Bacon trusted that knowledge of second causes could only heighten the dependence upon the First Cause. Just as Defoe seems to have found his own ideas about the religious preconditions of knowledge expressed by Bacon, so too he agreed with one of the major impulses of Bacon's philosophy, namely, an awareness that excessive order and regularity had been attributed traditionally to nature. For example, Defoe upheld Copernicus's criticism of the Ptolemaic astronomical system. Indeed, Defoe vehemently disparaged the notion that the celestial bodies move in circles and championed Copernicus because the latter validated his ideas with rational proofs. Defoe willingly conceded that the new philosophy made certain biblical notions redundant and required a slightly modified attitude toward the Scriptures.[11] His contempt for the conservative reaction against Copernicus constitutes one example of his sympathy with progressive thinking; it has a lot in common with Bacon's Idols of the Tribe. Defoe defends Copernicus against the ignorant self-sufficiency which allows men to feel themselves the measure of creation.

Defoe's support of the Copernican astronomical system also has affinities with one of the major aims of Bacon's scientific method, namely, the exposure of selective spiritualization of nature. Bacon promoted a thoroughly empirical attitude towards nature and tried to give science a theoretical independence from religion partly because of his awareness that nature was regarded commonly in an arbitrarily figurative way. Despite his claim that increased knowledge of nature improves religious sense and rules out the possibility of atheism, Bacon was obliged to argue as if the truths of nature and the Bible are dual. Interestingly, although he agreed with Bacon about the arbitrarily figurative way in which nature was regarded, Defoe developed a dual attitude towards nature in order to show that it is impossible to separate theory of knowledge from religious assumptions. In *The Storm*, his account of the spectacular tempest of 1703, Defoe maintains that the winds are one of the phenomena which God has reserved as a means of directly admonishing mankind. As such, he insists, they are not susceptible to scientific hypothesis. Most natural phenomena could be analyzed by cause-and-effect reasoning because God in setting the course of things in motion and in guiding nature with the 'Executive Power' of providence had rendered the creation accessible to human anlysis (p. 2). In such analysis there was no need to inquire after God because the natural course of things was 'plain and demonstrative' in testifying to divine control. But when the causes were indiscernible, as in the case of the winds, the only possible conclusion was that God's purpose was to prevent rational inquiry and to resolve the matter into 'Speculation.' By this word Defoe means meditation. His point is that nature always directs attention beyond itself to the divine and that the general and particular operation of providence makes it impossible to ignore the consideration that knowledge always leads to religious sense. That is, when knowledge of nature is attainable, it is transparent with divine truth, and, when knowledge of nature is impossible, the impossibility alerts the inquirer to spiritual exercise. Knowledge could not be restricted to natural causes because nature is not self-contained and because certain causes are to be discovered only through faith. In Defoe's mind, the man of faith, aided by grace and revelation, is enabled to conceive of creation holistically, whereas the mere philosopher, able to consider second causes and fact solely, has no prerogative in the realm of value and morality.

> The Christian begins just where the Philosopher ends; and when the Enquirer turns his Eyes up to Heaven, Farewel Philosopher; 'tis a Sign he can make nothing of it here. (p. 6)

To Defoe the storm recalled Christ's words in John III, 8: *'The Wind blows where it listeth, and thou hearest the Sound thereof, but knowest not whence it cometh'* (p. 10). Not only does Christ's statement refer to man's fallibility but also it is an analogy to the mystery of spiritual rebirth. Defoe cites this verse to support his contention about the relation of ultimate truth and religious sense. Yet his citation is also an act of meditation. However, although he distinguishes between the relative scope of the philosopher and the Christian, that can denominate Bacon a Christian philosopher indicates his desire to consider religious sense in tension with empirical knowledge and science rather than simply in opposition to it.

If, on account of his religious sense, Defoe could tolerate and even assimilate Baconian empiricism, he stood firm against the rational optimism of the Cartesian tradition. He found the method of rational introspection associated with *'Cogito, ergo sum'* unacceptable. Consequently, he judged Descartes's disciple, Malebranche, to be one whose philosophic flights had taken him into unintelligible fantasies.[12] The mathematical basis of Cartesian rationalism must have seemed objectionable to Defoe, given his belief that philosophers who pored 'upon the Sacred Mysteries of Religion with the Mathematical Engines of Reason' could produce only 'incoherent Stuff' by way of conclusions.[13] Certainly, Defoe worried about the extent to which Christians turned to rationalism to understand their faith.

> 'Tis strange to think that Men professing Christianity, should condemn every Doctrine that comes not within the Reach of their own shallow capacities; in them as Christians, 'tis the most amazing Insolence and Folly to affirm, that those Things of which we can frame no perfect Idea, that we can't comprehend and bring down to the Standard of human Reason, are irrational Absurdities.[14]

To defend his belief in religious sense, Defoe urges that human reason is not the full measure of reason. He emphasizes the positivistic and reductive aspects of rationalism in order to suggest how they inevitably serve to support deism and atheism. His understanding of fallibility made the rationalist's tenet that the mind can attain a perfect idea seem glib and implausible. Defoe was convinced that neither *a priori* definitions nor rational standards can have a direct bearing on matters of faith. Hence, he declared it morally dangerous *'to imagine, that bare Reason, unassisted by any other Help, is sufficient to fathom all the Depths of the Oracles of God.'* Rational perspicuity was not a criterion that could be applied single-mindedly to faith. For Defoe, the Scriptures were not intended to possess clear and distinct ideas in the Cartesian sense. Therefore, 'To prescribe to God how he ought to have revealed his Will, and to require those Things as necessary to divine Revelation, which Experience evinces not to have been complied with in the Christian, can only serve the Cause of Atheism.'[15] As far as Defoe was concerned, clear and distinct ideas could derive only from revelation and not from a rational method.

In his insistence that methodic doubt was irrelevant to the perception of religious ideas, Defoe adopted St. Paul's view that 'we now see but through a Glass darkly.' Thus, he could maintain that man can have no 'thorough knowledge of divine Mysteries' and he could gainsay Christian rationalists who sought to 'find out the Almighty to Perfection.' He reminded those who 'think to measure the Heavens with a Span, and vye with Omnipotence it self in Science' that they 'would do well to consider, that Things nearer and more familiar to us are so abstrusely concealed, that the most learned and ingenious Dissertations of the best Philosophers, are but as probable Conjectures, and far from arriving at a Demonstration.'[16] Although the rationalists adopted a method which aimed at a properly conditional form of knowledge, in Defoe's eyes they were more dogmatic than they realized because they did not recognize the disproportion between their ideas and the objects of their attention. Although his dislike of methodic doubt seems close to typical objections to Cartesian rationalism, namely, that when mathematics is not its object it engages in an impossible level of abstraction and that self-reflection cannot assure certainty unless there is some check on the introspective faculty, he also challenges rationalistic accounts of ordinary reality. Defoe holds that philosophers can do no more than speculate about many empirical matters and that rationalism cannot make familiar things transparent. In a way, Defoe's point is that much of ordinary reality is as far beyond the reach of rationalism as divine mysteries are: 'it is not only Things Divine and Spiritual, but Earthly and Temporal, that abundantly surpass our Reason or Imagination.' From Defoe's point of view, the rationalists, besides possessing a limited idea of existence, had a narrow way of reacting to being.

> *Cogito, ergo sum* is a prime Conclusion with Philosophers, who believed Thinking the most evident Proof of Being; our Words and Actions are likewise performed, as directed by our Thoughts; and yet how little, what less do we know of any Thing in Nature than of this Operation of the Soul? and yet how absurd would it be to say, that because I cannot comprehend or define how it is I think, I therefore do not think, or speak, or act, or exist? So that here lies the Difference between apprehending and comprehending: we know and are assured of many Things that we are unable to comprehend or account for.[17]

Clearly, Defoe did not agree with the Cartesian notion that thinking proves existence. He conceded that thinking may govern the individual's words and actions, but he insisted that thinking about words and actions conveys nothing precise about the nature of the soul. He simply refused to confuse the order of knowing with the order of being. From this viewpoint it is senseless to affirm that, because the processes of thought cannot be defined, they cannot exist. Indeed, Defoe is firm that neither mental processes nor the nature of the soul depend upon rational definitions. Rejecting the Cartesian duality of body and soul, Defoe assumes the common-sense position that the interaction of body and soul is necessary for everyday life. But, by denying that man can create a rationally objective standard by which to judge significant spiritual truths, Defoe had no intention of rendering these truths less immediate. On the contrary, he depreciated comprehension in order to appreciate apprehension. His insistence on the difference between knowing how and knowing that emphasizes the redundancy of the Cartesian process of introspection and points up the validity of the individual reaching truth by wondering at the relation of the material and immaterial, by puzzling over their unity, and by recognizing that knowledge and spiritual well-being depend on the association of body and soul. The Cartesian tradition represented to Defoe the reduction of religious experience to heterodox rationalism. His religious sense impelled him to argue that apprehension is sufficient for moral living and that comprehension is possible only through the agency of grace and revelation.

Defoe's orthodox reaction against rationalism shows that his estimation of religious sense was relatively undogmatic. What might be called the latitudinarian aspects of his religious sense are illustrated further by his admiration of Sir Thomas Browne. Defoe really did esteem Browne: he referred to him as a learned and pleasant author, the inimitable and merry doctor, and our late great scholar and physician.[18] On an occasion when he required support for his religious views upon sexual ethics, Defoe cited *Religio Medici* as a moral authority.[19] Doubtless, too, Browne's arguments in favour of religious toleration must have proved agreeable to Defoe, for Browne's claim that all who profess the basic Christian tenets are members of one Church[20] finds frequent echoes in Defoe's contention that, since the Dissenters are true to the Protestant creed, their faith as regards the requisites of salvation is identical to that of the Church of England.[21] Browne's dislike of sectarian strife and his efforts to render matters of faith more important than ecclesiastical or jurisdictional concerns must also have appealed to Defoe. One indication of this is the vehemence with which Crusoe is given to dismiss 'Niceties in Doctrines' and 'Schemes of Church Government' as irrelevant to faith. For Defoe, as well as for Crusoe, 'the disputed Points in Religion' have simply confused the world and bear no relation to the Christian's prime duty to attend to the Bible and the Holy Ghost.[22] In passing, it is interesting to note that Crusoe's rejection of his 'own private meer Reading' because it is spiritually inefficacious and his awareness that his inadequate teaching of Friday is properly self-instructive have much in common with Browne's position that by teaching one learns and by being committed to action one gains inner development.

Important to a consideration of Defoe's religious sense is his sharing with Browne the position that right action is difficult for fallen man. As a consequence of this position, Browne recognized the need to inculcate imperatives more categorical than human feelings. So, he stressed the notion of rewards and punishments together with belief in Heaven and Hell. Of particular significance is Browne's emphasis on the reality of the Devil. Browne depicted the Devil forcefully in order to defend the moral universe against the incursions of science and to prevent God from being distanced from the operation of creation. Defoe shared these impulses. In *The Political History Of The Devil* he maintains the importance of belief in Satan as an imperative to morality and faith.

> The Truth is, *God* and *the Devil*, however opposite in their nature, and remote from one another in their places of abiding, seem to stand pretty much upon a level in our faith: For as to our believing the reality of their existence, he that denies one generally denies both; and he that believes one necessarily believes both. (p. 302)

Clearly, for Defoe, the Devil's existence is a logical requirement of the moral order. Defoe is, however, very careful not to equate belief in the Devil with belief in God. He discriminates between belief in Satan which he sees as a debt owed to reason and belief in the Creator which he regards as a debt owed to nature. Similarly to Browne, Defoe presents Satan as a figure of despair and degradation: the Devil's negative will is contrasted with the positive goodness of God. Drawing somewhat on Milton as well, Defoe suggests that Satan is his own hell, that, although he dwells in men's hearts, he cannot destroy men, and that he is powerless to destroy himself. In Defoe's judgment, an individual will uphold the moral order only if he recognizes and conquers the devil in his own heart. Defoe's presentation of the Devil seems to derive from Browne not only its logical necessity but also the impulse to deflate superstitious accounts of evil. The Devil does not simply serve as an indirect proof of God's existence: he also fulfils the evangelical function of arousing people to mortification and penitence.

Defoe's religious sense can be understood further by comparing the ways in which he and Browne describe the aesthetic value of religious ideas. Both see, for instance, in spiritual harmony a way of celebrating the divine presence in the creation. To begin with, Browne regards harmony as the object of contemplation. For him, harmony is spiritual music, a sense of unity resulting from perception of order and proportion. According to Browne, the contemplative soul is bound to find the order of the heavens to be music and God to be the chief of composers. This is so because God reveals his divinity partly by accommodating the harmony of creation to the harmonical nature of man's soul. In a sense, Browne thinks of harmony as a mediator between the divine and the human: man can share in the harmony which sounds as intellectual idea in the ear of God.[23]

Defoe expresses similar attitudes towards harmony. With a keen sense of paradox, he views music as a terrestrial infinite. For him, music is a natural phenomenon immediately inspired from Heaven and far above human invention: music is the form of harmony with which God has suffused and unified the creation. Hence, harmony is

> all Proportions, all Symmetry of Parts and Connection of Circumstances, the original Beauty of Nature, the concurring Order of the Creation, the Obedience of Consequences to their causes, the Circulation of Seasons, Times, Heavenly and Earthly Bodies, the Subordination of Parts, Degrees and Things, and Secret Influences of Sovereign Power in the Determinations of all Human Affairs.

In Defoe's estimation, as in Browne's, harmony, in addition to addressing the eye as well as the ear, speaks to the meditative soul. Thus, while oratory and poetry can create an influential unison in the soul, Defoe is convinced that the same effect results from meditating on the life of a pious and just man.[24] But Defoe's ultimate proposition about spiritual harmony is that the beauty of the creation can be realized fully only by the eye of a religious beholder. That is, he maintains that revelation, as distinct from reason, is integral to aesthetic pleasure:

> The beauteous Works of Providence are all Musick to the observing Mind; when we view the Heaven, the Work of his Hand, the Moon and the Stars which he has made, what Musick is there, is the Contemplation.[25]

Defoe's final point in relation to harmony seems to be that not only is aesthetic appreciation dependent upon prior religious truths but also aesthetic appreciation is essentially worship of the divine. In his affinities with Browne, then, Defoe argues implicitly that religious sense involves the inseparability of aesthetics and knowledge and that it must be responsive to immanent religious truths.

Consideration of his similarities to Browne partly reveals the attitudes which underlie Defoe's search for the noumenal in the phenomenal, the holy in the world. Perhaps surprisingly, Defoe's religious sense can also be elucidated by an examination of his reactions to Thomas Hobbes. Despite Hobbes's atheism, Defoe was far from ignoring the notorious philosopher. Indeed, he regarded him as 'an exalted Spirit in Philosophy.'[26] Of course, Defoe did not sympathize with Hobbes's philosophical reliance upon Euclidian geometry and the new physics. He was especially intolerant of materialist notions of the soul. By arguing the common-sense position that there is an obvious distinction between life and matter, he denied Hobbes's equation of substance with body. Defoe also thought absurd the conclusion of Hobbes's thorough-going materialism, namely, that God is a corporeal spirit. Against what he took to be a contradiction in terms, Defoe asserted the reasonableness of immaterial substance and defended 'the *Immortality* as well as *Immateriality* of the Soul.'[27] Nor could Defoe have possibly agreed with Hobbes's attempt to explain ethics in terms of mechanical impulse and physiological motivation. It is commonly urged against Hobbes that he oversimplifies by treating as equivalent description of egotistical motives to action and prescription of moral value which renders action dutiful.[28] Defoe understood this objection to Hobbes, for he refused the notion that psychological compulsion possesses moral integrity. Hence, when Moll Flanders is driven by a 'riveted Aversion' to her brother, whom she accidentally marries, to act beyond 'right in point of Policy,' she recognizes that there can be no moral justification for her abuse of him because she had not been concerned with behaving towards her brother 'in point of Conscience.' For Defoe, the drive to aversion cannot be related necessarily to moral sense. He reinforces this point by making Moll herself stress that her account is 'of what was, not of what ought or ought not to be.'[29] When Crusoe affirms that 'All Motions to Good or Evil are in the Soul,' Defoe's refusal to concede a Hobbesian physiological basis to morality seems transparent.[30] Good and evil are not to be reduced to introspective awarenesses of vital motions. For Defoe the Christian moralist, virtue cannot be directly associated with the desires of appetite. He held to the imperative that rational impartiality is necessary to morality and he believed that in proper human thought is to be found impersonal truth. Hence, in depicting Moll's potential for repentance, Defoe insists that she can move away from her merely self-interested state of mind as a prisoner in Newgate.

> In short, I began to think, and to think is one real Advance from Hell to Heaven; all that Hellish harden'd state and temper of Soul, which I have said so much of before, is but a deprivation of Thought; he that is restor'd to his Power of thinking, is restor'd to himself.[31]

Moll suggests that through impersonal thinking the individual comes to a true sense of self. This implicit dialectic of impartial reasoning and individuality makes the Hobbesian notion that virtue can be described solely in terms of feelings and impulses appear naive and implausible. Through Moll, Defoe argues that being reasonable and thoughtful is a necessary prescription against complete self-interest and that it is also a form of religious self-preparation.

Although Defoe did not consider the passions as legitimate motivating forces, he applied some of Hobbes's attitudes towards human nature to his own purposes. Like Hobbes, for example, he believed in the uniformity of human nature and held psychological causes and effects to be universal and unchanging. Defoe also concurred with Hobbes that the passions degrade human dignity with what seems an inexorably malicious force.[32] But, whereas Hobbes made the anarchy of the passions the foundation of society and the justification of political absolutism, Defoe insisted that it is society's function to curb passions in a moral way. Consequently, Defoe would not regard natural or pre-political society as a model for the moral function which institutionalized society had to perform.

> Humane Nature is still the same; and to live in the unlimited Freedom of a *State* of *Nature*, would be attended still with all the same Inconveniencies and Mischiefs, that ever did attend it.[33]

The need for a religious understanding of the uniformity of human nature is a theme that is particularly evident in Crusoe's meditations about the willingness of primitive people to give up natural society and to adopt civilization. Crusoe concedes that it is wrong to question the providential dispensation which prevents primitive people from exercising their human potential. Yet, in recognizing that God has bestowed upon them 'the same Powers, the same Reason, the same Affections, the same Powers of Kindness and Obligation, the same Passions and Resentments of Wrongs, the same Sense of Gratitude, Sincerity, Fidelity, and all the Capacities of doing Good, and receiving Good' that the Europeans have received, Crusoe can only be struck by the relative ingratitude of the Europeans for the providential dispensation which allows them scope to exercise their capacities.[34] The salient point of Crusoe's meditation is that both the ingratitude of the Europeans and the eagerness of primitive people to adopt civilization demonstrate the basic importance of religious enlightenment to society and show that society will not restrict the passions unless it embodies religious sense.

On account of his religious stance toward human potential, Defoe did not accept Hobbes's claim that the state derives solely from the aggressive passions. Defoe would not agree that the passions universally degrade human dignity. Although, as in such works as *Jure Divino*, he relates the origin of government partly to crime, lust, and war, he did not equate the state of nature with the state of war, as Hobbes did. Defoe granted that all men might want power, but he maintained that they would not want it for the same acquisitive reason. He insisted on the strength of sexual and domestic passions, claiming that fondness for women and tenderness for offspring cannot be left out of any definition of the state of nature.

> From hence arise benign Dispositions, Softness of Temper and Friendships, these being more pleasant and safe than Quarrelling, and Fighting.

Defoe thought Hobbes absurdly wrong in his notion of the state of nature because he had ignored people's impulses to continue their enjoyment of life and to improve themselves.[35] Defoe, obviously, believed in natural sociable impulses which are not reducible to aggressive self-interest. Moll Flanders exemplifies this tenet when she acknowledges that maternal affection is placed by nature in women's hearts to prompt mothers to sacrifice themselves to the protection and care of their children. Although she stands self-condemned of 'intentional Murther' because she finds a foster mother for her own child, Defoe generates sympathy for her by indicating how much she is governed by circumstance. Sympathy is owed to Moll because of the very conflict between her material self-interest and the maternal dictates of the law of nature.[36]

Despite his various objections to Hobbes's reductive ideas, Defoe still exploited them for moral and religious purposes. For instance, motifs stemming from Hobbes's prescriptions for earthly happiness are evident in *Robinson Crusoe*. Hobbes defined happiness as the continuous attainment of objects for the satisfaction of ever increasing desires. Such happiness, depending entirely upon the conception of life as nothing much more than perpetual motion, Defoe regarded as illusory. Through Crusoe's experience on the island, Defoe shows that this shallow view of happiness does not elicit the best from a person. Crusoe's acquisition of things is in itself relatively valueless: it certainly does not ensure happiness. His reaction to the foot-step proves that material belongings are precarious and that happiness must be considered in relation to the 'uneven State of human Life.'

> To Day we love what to Morrow we hate; to Day we seek what to Morrow we shun; to Day we desire what to Morrow we fear; nay, even tremble at the Apprehension of.

Without the significance and security afforded by religious society, enjoyment is untenable. Indeed, because he is isolated, Crusoe is victimized by the 'secret moving Springs in the Affections.' His imaginative yearning for society is so great that he behaves automatically and his body cramps mechanically: 'that Motion carries out the Soul by its Impetuosity to such violent eager embracings of the Object, that the Absence of it is insupportable.'[37] Interestingly, to support his religious view of happiness and to discountenance a materialist view of happiness which has strong affinities with Hobbes's position, Defoe makes Crusoe experience distress in terms that are in accord with Hobbes's psychology of motion. It is as if Defoe draws upon some aspects of Hobbes's thought in order to attack others. Defoe's major concern, to promote a religious sense of happiness, is, however, embedded in Crusoe's unhappiness. That he does not control his passions results in providence leading him on a *'Wild Goose Chase'*; his farther adventures continue his unhappiness because he does not let religion and reason teach him to seek beyond 'human Enjoyments for a full Felicity.'[38]

In order to be prescriptive about religious sense, Defoe, in addition to criticizing implicitly Hobbes's notion of happiness, exploits the philosopher's reductive psychology. For example, Defoe's belief that life ought to be 'but one universal Act of Solitude' can be related to Hobbes's solipsism. For purposes of persuasion, Defoe countenances a Hobbesian view of perception and asserts that solipsism is the normal consequence of man's attention to the world. 'Every Thing revolves in our Minds by innumerable circular Motions, all centring in ourselves.' Defoe is sweeping in his claim that predispositions and prejudices structure the way in which individuals judge events and objects and in his declaration that perception usually leads to narrow and self-contained thinking. 'All Reflection is carry'd Home, and our Dear-Self is, in one Respect, the End of Living.' Defoe is prepared to admit that man is a lonely creature to whom the feelings and concerns of others are remote and even beyond apprehension.

> Our Meditations are all Solitude in Perfection; our Passions are all exercised in Retirement; we love, we hate, we covet, we enjoy, all in Privacy and Solitude. All that we communicate of those Things to any other, is but for their Assistance in the Pursuit of our Desires; the End is at Home; the Enjoyment, the Contemplation, is all Solitude and Retirement; 'tis for our selves we enjoy, and for our selves we suffer.

In this instance, Defoe's emphasis upon solipsism heightens his conviction that the only remedy is cultivation of the soul. He maintains that it is solely by taking care of the spirit that the individual can communicate essentially to himself and God. By stressing natural psychological isolation, Defoe tries to argue that it is morally necessary to transform it into a spiritual solitude. By accepting that solipsism proves men to be isolated from one another and detached from the world, Defoe can recommend as a natural remedy an ascetic restraint of thought and of desire and a reverence for revelation and grace.[39]

That Defoe applied a religious interpretation to solipsism is in accord with the reservations he expressed about Hobbes's view of self-interest and the acquisitive passions. In Defoe's eyes, Hobbes's emphasis on self-interest made the philosopher's definition of 'the State of human Felicity ... a strange, precarious, odd, disagreeable Thing.' In rejecting this emphasis, Defoe maintained that self-interest induced people in all levels of society to commit deeds which were 'inconsistent with the ordinary Rule of Living, and inconsistent with the usual Power of the Passions and Affections.'[40] Self-interest, far from advancing human nature, was potentially dangerous because it could cause men to forget about justice, honesty, and the last judgment. Moreover, Defoe argued, nothing a man in society does can have repercussions only upon himself, so that if an individual ventures for his own gain without the consent of those who might be affected by his actions, he must be judged criminal. As well as being critical about Hobbes's individualistic assumptions, Defoe attacked the sorts of rationalization of moral responsibility which self-interest necessarily prompts. Hence, Defoe claims that self-interested individuals attribute their failures to fate and their successes solely to their own agency. Displeased by such moral evasiveness, Defoe agreed with Machiavelli that men should be coerced into seeing their social and moral duty if prevented from doing so by selfishness. To Defoe it seemed justifiable on prudential and social grounds that men of enterprise should have their self-interest limited.[41] Those who, ignoring a spiritual perspective, reduced everything, including friendship, to a matter of self-interest Defoe regarded as cynics. Consequently, he cited Rochester's lines *'In my dear Self I centre every Thing, / My God, my Soul, my Country, and my King,'* since they well represented to him that unacceptable state of contemporary society in which friendly obligations were no longer reliable and the ungrateful reaction to benefactors threatened the continuation of charity. Certainly, Defoe was prepared to explain the dominance of self-love in Hobbesian terms.

> *Self*, in a Word, governs the whole World; the present Race of Men all come into it. 'Tis the foundation of every prospect in Life, the beginning and end of our Actions; and where those Actions, at any Time, do not answer this End, they are so far eccentrick and out of square. 'Tis to move retrograde to the general System of Life; and to stand as it were by ourselves.

But this descriptive stance allows Defoe to imply the need for moral courage in order to withstand the prevalence of self-interest. For, selfishness he equates with the archetypal sin against God, and he suggests that, if self-interest becomes morally acceptable as a principle of life, man and society will degenerate to the point of becoming devilish.[42]

Inasmuch as Defoe concurred with Hobbes's notion that self-love is rooted in mankind, as, for instance, when he acknowledged that it 'too often escapes from us in our Discourse, and betrays us before we are aware,' his descriptions of self-love are transformed into occasions for celebrating religious sense. This is so partly because he did not concede that self-interest was by definition evil. Although he insisted that it is equally wicked to omit concern for others who find themselves in a crisis as to exploit their misfortune, he thought it allowable for people themselves in a crisis to be concerned for themselves rather than for others. Defoe, therefore, admitted the necessity of self-interest in certain circumstances, but he made it a matter of moral attitude as distinct from an issue of action and conduct. Not surprisingly, he firmly rejected La Rochefoucauld's Hobbesian notion that all behaviour can be reduced to simple self-interest. Indeed, he attributed La Rochefoucauld's maxim to a lazy generalization of merely individual values. Defoe himself refused to estimate human nature too low. His tenet that every virtue borders on a vice made him hold that self-love could be virtuous as well as vicious. La Rochefoucauld's maxims in giving 'the worst Turn to every Thing' might reflect penetration but their lack of discrimination revealed their author's want of good nature. Not only did Defoe maintain that the individual can serve his country and his neighbours with integrity even as he serves himself but also he insisted that the individual can intend the good of others as an end in itself, that is, without expecting to benefit himself. Clearly, Defoe believed it to be honest, humane, and charitable for the analyst of human nature to respect the integrity of intention and to accept the reality of goodness in society. 'I had rather ascribe it to a general Complacency and Good-will to our Fellow-Creatures, than to Vanity and Ostentation.'[43] As is demonstrated by his use of some of Hobbes's reductive ideas for rhetorical purposes, Defoe held that the social commentator ought to put the best possible construction on things which can be improved by religious rules and conduct. Consequently, he felt himself obliged to apply the truths of the Christian dispensation in order to illumine partly enlightened ideas and to prove that the latter were consistent with divine purposes.

Even when he felt contempt for a given philosopher, Defoe did not let his feelings prevent him from taking the opportunity to promote his notion of religious sense. For example, Defoe found nothing positive to say about John Toland, the notorious champion of deism. But, despite his contemptuous allusions to Toland, Defoe was able to be constructive in expressing his views about the social and doctrinal effects of deism. To Defoe, Toland was not just wicked; he was also 'a Heritick of prostituted Principles.'[44] On one occasion he refers to the deist as 'the Learned (to say nothing else of him,) Mr. *Toland*' and continues by declaring that, since nothing should be said about the dead unless it is good, he will not comment further.[45] This restraint is wholly ironical, for Defoe viewed Toland as someone who had misused his learning 'to shock the Faith of Christians in the glorious Person and Divinity of their Redeemer, and to sap and undermine the Principles and Foundations of the orthodox Faith.'[46] Defoe was disgusted by Toland not only because the latter had applied reason to the detraction of the Trinity but also because this misapplication of reason was really an appeal to social pride and fashionable self-conceit. Indeed, Defoe claimed that Toland had inspired the foundation of atheistical clubs and societies and that his success proved his sense of reason to be relative and modish rather than general and absolute. On account of his orthodox sense of moral imperatives, Defoe was appalled to consider that the mockery of religion in certain social clubs included the design 'to erase the natural awe of a Sovereign Creator out of the Hearts of Men.' Hence, far from ignoring Toland after death, Defoe was pleased to speculate that Toland's reportedly violent end testified to providence's ordinary and natural course of vindicating moral truth. That the enemy of revealed religion, the opposer of orthodox principles, and the blasphemer of Christ's divinity had been made an example was, for Defoe, only to be expected.

Defoe regarded Toland as a man of 'pretended Philosophy,' since the effect of deism was to reduce the certain and the conceptual to the vague and the hypothetical. Defoe judged it merely sophistical that deists should try to distinguish

> Principles into Notions, and Doctrines into Moot Points, ... God himself into a Deity and no Deity, our Blessed Saviour into a mere Man-Redeemer, and the Holy Spirit into a Non-Entity, not to be talk'd any more of.[47]

He could not conceive of separating 'the undivided Nature of an infinite Self-existent Being' into superior and inferior classes because he was convinced that such logical differentiation was irrelevant to creed and faith. For Defoe, the deists' invasion of the 'religious Constitution' with logic and reason was evidence that they were entirely ignorant of the nature of belief and religious doctrine. He was sure that their rationalization of religion had failed to produce a new norm of faith and that they had merely reintroduced the heresies of Arius and Socinus. In addition to harming the established church, the deists had brought about a new sectarianism which, in order to attack Toland more sharply, Defoe distinguished from former schisms: he felt that, whereas earlier schisms had arisen through unrestrained religious fervour, the sectarianism of the deists derived solely from self-interested scorn of virtue and religion.

With his supposed rationalism Toland had tried to persuade people that he was intent on promoting religious toleration and overcoming sectarianism.

But Defoe recognised this promotion of toleration as a direct assault on religious sense and fundamental doctrine. Toland had 'Panegyrickt the *Jews* and *Mahometans* as Good Christians, and proposed a Comprehension of them all together into Christ's Church.'[48] Defoe felt justified in seeing this sort of toleration as a new heterodox sectarianism. In this sort of toleration he perceived an effort to overthrow the doctrine of salvation as preached by Christ and handed down by apostles and ministers 'upon whose Preaching the Holy Ghost has stampt his Authority by the evident Operations of its Power Concurring with it, to turn the Souls of Men from Darkness to Light.' Obviously, Defoe's dislike of Toland stems partly from respect for the integrity of the Christian communion and traditional doctrine. Toland also earned Defoe's contempt on account of his rejection of Christ's divinity and place in the Trinity. In reaction, Defoe insisted upon the orthodox view of Christ's nature, 'viz., the Equality of Power, the Unity of Substance of Jesus Christ the Son with his *Father, the Almighty Creator of Heaven and of Earth.*' Because Toland denigrated St. Paul and rejected original sin, Defoe could not endure his name and felt impelled to think of the deist as an archetypal hypocrite who had disguised his life in order to 'pretend true Religion, and yet profess Heresy; to talk as a Protestant, and yet worship as a *Socinian.*'[49] As an orthodox Christian, Defoe held that Adam's Fall had brought about 'a Natural Propensity in us to do Evil' with the result that human nature was possessed of 'no Natural Inclination to do Good.' He maintains, in a way that reveals his reliance upon St. Paul, that this *'Indwelling Sin'* obliges man to look beyond himself for salvation and to acknowledge his inability to overcome the discrepancy between intention and conduct. Against the position of rationalists and deists Defoe cited St. Paul: *'To Will is present with me, but how to perform that which is good I know not: In me, that is, in my flesh dwelleth no good thing.'* Unlike Toland, Defoe considered that the gap between the ideal and the actual was central to moral living and that the only way to confront original sin was through obedience to Christ. Hence, drawing upon St. Paul Defoe can assert that *'there is now no Condemnation to them which are in Christ Jesus.'*[50] Defoe's belief in revelation and in the necessity of divine mystery is obviously more consistent with orthodoxy than with deistic rationalization of creed. So, it is not surprising that the hypothetical imperative of reason which concerned Toland should be judged by Defoe as irrelevant to Christian obedience. For Defoe, only the transcendent truth of Christ could effect religious sense.

Although he was more temperate in his reaction to the Earl of Shaftesbury than he was to Toland, Defoe nevertheless felt impelled to criticize Shaftesbury's deistic concepts from the point of view of religious sense. The separation of morality and religion and the theory of moral sense were two aspects of deism which particularly bothered Defoe and which prompted him to argue that an interested, as distinct from impassive, creator was essential to morality. Defoe agreed with Shaftesbury's notion that the individual can be moral only if he possesses an awareness of social good. But, for Defoe, this condition, while necessary, was not sufficient. Consequently, unlike Shaftesbury, Defoe maintained that a man would not become an honest subject and neighbour unless he were to recognize that absolute religious truth alone endows an awareness of social good with imperative authority. That 'the Good of the whole ought to be preferred before the Good of any private Person' is 'because 'tis the Voice of Nature, and therefore the Will of the God of Nature.'[51] Since he assumed that moral sense meant little if conceived independently of religious sense, Defoe believed that love for the human race was not adequate to oblige a man to act humanely and to fulfil covenants. While he conceded that the recognition of the prior good of society might be a natural dictate, he insisted that, as such, it testified to the absoluteness of divine commitment to human society. As a result, Defoe could emphasize that it was inconsistent of deists, who do not believe in a personal god, to claim to bind themselves to duties the sole sanction for which is a sympathetic creator. He was convinced that, by defining God as impassive and impersonal, the deists had rejected the possibility of moral priority. Defoe was equally sure that a deist had no right to expect orthodox people to credit that he would put the public before his private interest since, if he acted contrariwise, he could not anticipate being called to account for himself by God. Defoe himself was clear that the individual would perform good deeds only under the prospect of eternal rewards and punishments. He stressed this tenet partly on account of his realization that even those who trust to divine judgment are still inclined by human nature to prefer their own good to that of society. For Defoe, Shaftesbury's sense of humanity by itself possessed no imperative force and it was inevitable that the deist 'must in every thing, act as if he alone were to be happy, even by the Ruine of all others.'

Defoe's examination of the imperative force of the sense of humanity reveals the extent to which in his mind religious assumptions and faith inform the nature of moral action.

> Now, by Humanity, is meant the Performance of those things which are not owing upon any Covenant, express or implicit, but only and purely by Force of that common Obligation Nature lays upon all Men; 'tis the doing good Offices to another, which he cannot demand as strictly his Right, though a Duty from the other. Thus a good Man considers his Neighbour as related to himself, in as much as they are both the Creatures of the same

Creator; or that the natural and necessary Dependance of one Man upon another, proves it the Will of our common Father, that we should be mutually assistant; but neither of these Considerations can be of Force with the Atheist or Deist.

Obviously, Defoe considered that, because the deists did not regard God as the father of mankind, they could not respect other people as their fellow creatures. He thought their concept of humanity morally redundant because detached from religious analogies and implications. He firmly denied the possibility of 'good Nature' and 'a Sense of Honour' substituting for the 'higher Principles': from his point of view, people such as Shaftesbury who relied upon natural dictates were trusting merely to 'Humour and unaccountable Fancy.'[52] Nor could deists justify their conduct by indicating their respect for legal justice, for Defoe argued that religious justice involved a dependence upon divine will and that the individual who looked forward to life after death for the judgment of his conduct on earth was made more aware of the intrinsic value of his actions than he would be if he accepted the standards of civil justice only. In Defoe's mind, one could comply with legal justice and still be a villain since such civil standards ignored the idea of a personal god, whereas this was less likely to be the eventuality for the individual who possessed a religious respect for divine justice.

On account of his religious sense Defoe resisted the influence which some of Shaftesbury's ideas exercised upon education. Indeed, Defoe held that human progress and individual development could happen only if they were based on a relation to God and universal truths. Genius, wit, and other natural capacities were valuable in themselves, but Defoe preferred to estimate them as if they were jewels which required polishing. This necessary improvement had to be effected by religious instruction since 'the dictates of nature are not the best guides.' Defoe, then, rejected Shaftesbury's tenet that the unguided inclination chooses wisely and resists sensuous pleasure. In maintaining that the will requires both instruction and example before it can choose morally, Defoe opposes original sin to natural morality. His conviction that 'nature is originally deprav'd' made him impatient with learned talk about 'the rectitude of Nature and of natural religion.' As far as Defoe was concerned, the natural impulses could provide no moral knowledge by themselves because men are 'hurry'd down the stream of their worst affections by the meer insensible impetuosity of nature.' He argued that virtue, far from being attained by introspective processes and feelings in the way claimed by Shaftesbury, had to derive from a balance of private and public interest which could be effected only by education in religion and the religious function of society. Whereas Shaftesbury believed man to be born a social creature with connatural ideas of right and wrong, Defoe insisted that the individual would achieve moral growth only by recognizing the necessity of experiencing society upon orthodox religious terms.[53]

Not surprisingly, Defoe attacked the kind of primitivism which Shaftesbury promoted. His religious sense of society made Defoe ready to defend social life as an important means of improving human nature. Nor did he regard the comforts of society as insignificant since he held the social environment to be instrumental to ethical intention and moral living. Consequently, while Shaftesbury eulogized natural man on the supposition of his being free from the vices of European civilization, Defoe tended to be scornful about primitive life. In Defoe's conception, natural man was inevitably wild, naked, dumb, and used to a vegetative existence unacceptable to many animals. Since, according to Defoe, natural man was necessarily dull in his senses, his lack of rational society also made him unaware of such basic impulses as self-preservation. Primitive man was simply an object of "MERE uninformed NATURE, a Life wanting a Name to distinguish it, like a Creature abandoned by Nature itself, and left in a State worse than that of the Sensitive Part of the Creation.' Defoe went further in criticizing natural man by suggesting that an individual who grows up outside society seems not even to possess a soul, the reason being that distinctively human faculties exist and develop only in an accommodating social environment. Defoe believes, therefore, that human nature must be refined by the experience and instruction which only a society true to religious principles can afford. Defoe also contends that the primitive man knows neither good nor evil while, as soon as he enters society, he experiences self-interest and demonstrates a predilection for vice; natural man, then, testifies to original sin and to the fact that society is the real agent of moral knowledge. Defoe's slighting treatment of primitive man shows how limited he thought moral sense was. As far as he was concerned, because society with a Christian constitution was best able to furnish the individual with moral education, no one ought to entertain a primitive ideal of ethics.[54]

Defoe's reaction to Shaftesbury is another example of how convinced he was that religion is the bond of virtue in this world and of how strongly he believed that revelation is the true sanction of moral law. But Defoe is not rigidly dogmatic. Despite his ideological distrust of Shaftesbury, he employed notions which derive from Shaftesbury, but he ensured that such notions fitted into his own religious perspective. Hence, although he rejected the moral arguments of primitivistic thinking, he did idealize savages from time to time as a means of commenting on the failings of European society.[55] In *An Attempt Towards a Coalition of English Protestants*, which amounts to an ardent plea for religious toleration of the Dissenters, Defoe at one point pretends that an atheist can act from a principle of simple morality for his country's as well as his own good. He does not, however, actually recommend atheist politicians, for he recognizes that usually they will be vicious. What, in essence, he does in order to urge that religious beliefs should not be subject to political discrimination is to emphasize that religion and politics are activities of different status and that they require different mental stances. This seemingly positive use of natural morality simply serves a specific, local effect: the rest of the work clearly shows that Defoe believed religion to be the sanction of politics and that he expected politicians to have Christian morality in the back of their minds as they discussed ideas relevant to religion and the constitution. While, then, to uphold his argumentative point that civil rights should not depend on religious rites Defoe adopts natural morality, he is equally insistent that charity and a religious sense ought to inform the political process in anticipation of the day of judgment when the importance of religious morality will finally be ascertained because every individual will be obliged to ask 'whether I have serv'd God according to the Dictates of my own Conscience, regulated by the Prescripts of *Holy Writ*?'[56]

CHAPTER 2

Natural and Divine Law

Reason is the Rule of Life to Man, as Religion is to Christians, he that is not guided by the last is an Infidel, as he that is not governed by the first is a Brute.

Where the Laws are Silent, there the general Rules of Reason and Religion take Place, and are Laws to Christians and to Men of Reason.[1]

Although Defoe considered the nature of morality from an orthodox religious perspective, for persuasive reasons he did not always exercise his judgment of particular moral issues from the point of view of religious sense. In his capacity as a moralist Defoe realized that he would be less effective if he were seen as someone perpetually intent on cajoling his readers with religious standards. An awareness of the rhetorical necessity of varying moral imperatives led him to appear to judge particular issues sometimes according to natural, as distinct from religious, standards. But he was ambivalent about the use of natural standards. While he was occasionally eager to reach the secular attitudes of his audience by appealing to natural principles, at other times he regretted having to rely on such standards because of the moral dangers which arguments founded on natural principles entailed. In his employment of natural law, then, Defoe is, on the one hand, energetic, committed, contemporary, and descriptive, and, on the other hand, melancholic, ambivalent, traditional, and prescriptive. There can be little doubt, however, that, on account of his concern for man's earthly and heavenly welfare, he recognized the value of appealing to natural law as one way of offsetting the inadequacies of civil law. In addition, he certainly believed that in the areas of marital relations, political mores, and social attitudes, to which civil legislation is inapplicable, there was considerable scope for introducing rules and regulations, and he assumed frequently that an appeal to natural law was one valid way of extending the implications of Christian ethics into those unlegislatable domains. Defoe, then, was willing to establish certain moral rules by considering what would convince the rational man in contradistinction to the Christian. That is, he was prepared to define a rule of life which was human because it was not bestial and to consider this human rule of life as parallel

30

to, but different from, a religious rule of life. But he was not always ready to distinguish between the grounds and arguments that would persuade the rational man and the Christian. Indeed, he often speaks of the rules of reason and religion as co-ordinate and equivalent. One can surmise, therefore, that, when Defoe differentiated between the appeal to reason and religion, he employed natural law as a rhetorical device to convey traditional values in contexts where it did not seem feasible to make traditional religious arguments, and that, when he regarded the dictates of natural law from a more abstract viewpoint, he would not conceive of the rules of reason independently of religion but, rather, viewed the status and authority of the former as wholly dependent on the latter.

Defoe's exposition of divine and natural imperatives is particularly interesting in *Conjugal Lewdness*, a work in which he set out to promote awareness of the necessity of restraint and regulation in the sexual conduct of married people. One of his initial concerns in this work was to discourage people from behaving as if the standards of civil law constituted a complete guide to moral action. For he held that civil law allowed certain impermissible forms of sexual license.

> What Excuse can it be to say, that the Law cannot reach it? Are there not many Sins which the Commands of GOD prohibits and forbids, which notwithstanding no Law can punish. (pp. 264-5)

In Defoe's mind, the standards of divine law were far more rigorous and precise than those of civil law. That earthly justice could not implement divine law proved to Defoe that true moral value could be realized only by the individual conscience. This explains his basic assumption that the moral conscience must guide itself by imperatives that society's laws are incapable of embodying. But, since the sexual misdeeds which he wished to proscribe were not declared by divine law to be sins, Defoe had to turn to natural law for an adequate set of positive dictates. His reliance upon natural law in this matter, however, did not entail setting aside consideration of either religion or society. The silence of the Scriptures about the sexual misconduct which he wished to outlaw obliged him to acknowledge that God had not needed to be explicit about this sort of misbehaviour because within the sound instincts of the human species as found in various societies were to be discovered natural imperatives which of themselves countered the sexual impulse and the immoral distortions it imposed upon mankind.

> The Crimes I attack are not only Offences against Heaven, but against all good Men, against Society, against Humanity, against Virtue, against Reason, and, in some Things, against Nature. (p. 401)

Obviously, Defoe does not rely on abstract principles of natural law alone for his condemnation of sexual indecencies. He is cautious about calling upon purely natural imperatives. Rather he seems to have believed it possible for individuals to arrive at a sense of the necessity of regulating sexual behaviour out of respect for moral conduct which fortifies society, supports the dignity of human nature, and serves the individual's best interest.

For Defoe, each individual, as a 'rational Creature,' was capable of recognizing the prudence of sexual discipline.

> If the Man is himself, if he is Master of his Reason, and sound Argument can make any due Impression upon him, he will consider this Part for his own sake; abstracted from its being an Offence against his Superior, the Governor of his Life, to whom he must account. (p. 392)

In this explanation of the individual's moral self-realization Defoe emphasizes rational response to argument rather than a precise train of religious or natural ideas. To Defoe's way of thinking, the individual must be fully himself through the aid of reason before he can respond to moral doctrine. Once the individual is rationally himself, he is enabled to consider moral arguments abstractly, that is, without needing to think in terms of ultimate religious imperatives. Needless to say, he still relies upon religious assumptions, but his sense of personal wholeness and of conformity with the condition of humane existence rests upon social and natural imperatives. These secular rules oblige him to be committed to sexual discipline and to admit that 'Nature calls for it, whether Religion calls for it or no' (p. 316). Of course, there is for Defoe no moral possibility of the individual's forgetting that he is accountable to God. Rather he contends that each person may find in the process of being true to himself and to humanity natural imperatives that are sufficient for the regulation of sexual behaviour.

The rhetorical and moral conditions under which Defoe respected this apparently naturalistic perspective are exemplified in his disapproving account of the habit of continuing intercourse after conception. He rejected the popular notion that custom in such matters acquires the force of law and unequivocally subordinated custom to natural law: 'Custom is a Tyrant; Nature is a just and limited Government' (p. 299). This political imagery not only depreciates all sense of legitimacy or necessity that might be thought to justify the habit he is assailing but also gives a constitutional, social, and public perspective to natural law. That is to say, the imagery reveals that Defoe discountenances primitivistic estimations of natural law and that he tends to see natural law in conventional and traditional moral terms. Indeed, Defoe usually considers natural law in relation to the Christian dispensation.

For example, he found it possible to claim that the unformulated rules of decency and sexual restraint are as binding upon the Christian as if they had been articulated in the decalogue, whereas he could not regard the Jewish laws which specifically ordered the separation of husband and wife after conception as absolute commands upon the conscience. For Defoe, the Jewish laws lacked a proper imperative since they were constituted only by custom and tradition while 'the Separation is evidently directed by the Law of Nature; 'tis directed from the first Principles of that knowledge which the most Ignorant are furnished with of themselves' (p. 326). Natural laws were binding to the conscience because, unlike custom and tradition, they represented to Defoe an immediate and basic moral knowledge which was established at creation. Hence, Defoe was confident that there is an implicit harmony between human nature and reason as a consequence of which sexual impulses to aversion and restraint possess the status of natural principles even in ignorant people. Clearly, he maintained that knowledge in the sense of intellectual awareness and positive rational judgment is not instrumental to these impulses, although knowledge understood as an intellectual check and a negative rational judgment is germane:

> The Law I am speaking of, is Nature, suported by Reason; or, if you please, Reason supported by Nature. Reason thinks it just to follow where Nature leads, and where there is no just and rational Objection against her Dictates, because Nature is certainly judge of her own Constitution, and best knows her own Actings; her Influences run in secret Channels, which no Force ought to obstruct, and, when they do not swell beyond Bounds, ought not to be check'd and stop'd up. (p. 300)

To the extent that logical priority is irrelevant to their relation, reason and nature are complementary. They are also reciprocal in the sense that reason must respect the organic knowledge that nature stands for, although as the checking and balancing faculty it may have to oppose itself to nature's dictates. The underground river imagery demonstrates Defoe's belief in the unalterable and elemental quality of natural impulses: through the imagery Defoe contends that the natural instincts exist beyond the scope of rational analysis but that their operation can be corrected by reason if they exceed their limits. On the one hand, then, Defoe sees immediate and universal imperatives within human nature while, on the other hand, he acknowledges that such imperatives are necessarily neither infallible nor irresistible. That is, Defoe does not go so far as to argue that the natural impulses have an absolute appeal or that they are unaffected by original sin:

> To be ignorant of a thing that Nature dictates, is shutting the Eyes against natural Light; resisting the most powerful Motive that can be found

opposing it. Why do not such People open their Eyes? Nature assists them to do it; but the debauched Inclination will fully close them; so that the Ignorance is really as criminal as the Action. (p. 313)

The corruption of disposition and the laziness of will accounted to Defoe for people being unaware of natural impulses, avoiding natural understanding, and evading natural imperatives. Such mental sloth, because it constituted unresisting subjection to original sin, Defoe thought as reprehensible as any specific sin. Connected, then, inseparably to Defoe's celebration of natural impulses is his qualification of their power by religious assumptions. This qualification demonstrates his estimation of the relative, as distinct from absolute, appeal of natural law and his concern for the religious inwardness of moral responsibility.

That the individual's acknowledgment of original sin is a precondition for the valid appeal to natural law is one clue to Defoe's religious understanding of natural imperatives. Another clue is his regret about reason's vulnerability before the senses, for this awareness of rational weakness indicates that Defoe's notion of the harmony between human nature and reason was prescriptive rather than descriptive:

Ungoverned Man! neither influenced by the Laws of God, or of Nature, gives a loose to his corrupted Desires, and subjects Nature, Reason, and even Religion it self, to his Appetite. (p. 295)

Since, for Defoe, self-discipline was problematical, neither divine nor natural law could exert an absolutely effective moral appeal. The dominance of the passions and the prevalence of fallibility meant that there could be nothing inherently more powerful in the imperative force of natural impulses than there was in that of religion. It appears, then, that on the ground of original sin there was at least some sort of negative equivalence between natural and divine law. Yet, more positively, Defoe frequently insisted that their dictates were identical. Often one encounters such statements as 'Nature and the Laws of God require it' (p. 12), 'There are Laws and Limits plac'd by Nature, nay, let me say, by the GOD of Nature, even to the conjugal Embraces' (p. 29), 'I am far from adding to the Restraints that Nature, and the GOD of Nature have laid upon us, but am for shewing you what Restraints they are' (p. 47). In such instances Defoe reminds his readers that the requirements of natural and divine law are reciprocal and interdependent. But, if for rhetorical reasons Defoe considers 'the general Rules of Reason' together (p. 229), there is other rhetorical evidence which suggests that he was unwilling to consider natural law independently of divine law.

Even in passages in which he resolves to adhere to natural imperatives, it is possible to detect the strain which Defoe experienced in attempting to regard natural law on its own terms. For instance, following a denunciation of contraception as an immoral action in itself, Defoe spontaneously claims that this sin is also contrary to 'several stated Rules of Life, which are of divine Institution.' Even though he retracts this religious stance hurriedly (p. 163), his desire to justify natural standards by divine ones is transparent. Likewise, when he decries premarital sexual intercourse, he condemns it as inconsistent with nature and common sense 'not to say a Word about Religion or the Laws of God' (p. 289). With reluctance he concedes that his audience will tolerate neither the mention nor the assumption of a religious perspective. But Defoe purposefully dramatizes his unhappiness with this situation, and, while he restrains himself from promoting the real imperative, he actually hints at its ultimate validity. His self-dramatization is not only, therefore, a matter of emotional appeal; it is also a form of ironical rhetorical deliberation. He appears as if he forlornly believes that he is compromising himself and as if he is obliged to be more worldly and less principled than he wants to be. As a consequence, his religious sense is inescapable.

Defoe's discontent at relying upon natural imperatives stems partly from his double estimate of natural law. Although, sometimes, he talks as if the laws of nature are stamped on the minds of reasonable humans with the result that, when civil and divine laws are silent, natural laws permit the individual to follow his reason which thereby becomes a divine law (pp. 87-88), Defoe held that, since natural law had been affected by the Fall, it could provide no unambivalent standard of judgment. Thus, he explained sexual promiscuity to be what 'Nature her self abhors, tho' Nature vitiated may be said to be the Occasion of it; I say, Nature, under any just Regulation of Sense, Nature, abstracted from criminal Habits, abhors it' (p. 62). The process of abstraction to which nature must be subjected is clearly based on the assumption of original sin, so that at least to this limited extent natural morality is relative to religious values. But Defoe's understanding of original sin led him to see that there need be no inevitable harmony between absolute and relative natural law.

> It is evident in many Cases, too many, had it not pleased GOD to suffer it to be so, that the Laws of Nature have a much stronger Influence upon us than the Laws of our Maker; and this is especially remarkable in those Cases, where the Laws of Nature seem to give some Latitudes which the Laws of GOD, and Institutions of his Providence, have thought fit to limit and restrain. (p. 60)

The cause of Defoe's regret in this passage is the inherent clash between divine and relative natural law. Although they signify God's putting corrupt human nature to use, relative natural laws seem to Defoe to induce licence rather than to effect restraint. Clearly, Defoe would have preferred a negative as distinct from positive function for natural law. Having maintained elsewhere that divine and natural laws are equally morally ineffective because of natural depravity, here Defoe suggests that natural dictates provide motives to action more irresistibly than divine laws. His point is that, while religious laws are necessarily prohibitive, natural laws, instead of inevitably reinforcing divine rules, commonly serve to rationalize illicit actions. For Defoe, then, natural laws are relative not simply in contrast to divine laws: they are also relative because their function depends significantly upon their context. Certainly, Defoe never surrendered his position that in their most meaningful use natural laws deny opportunities for moral licence. For instance, he maintained that, while natural laws dictate propagation and are responsible for the sexual drive, as such they are neither sufficient nor complete, because necessitated by the dictation of propagation is the regulation of propagation according to divine law. Since Defoe deemed that the Fall had rendered the dictates to propagation relative, that is, had reduced them to impulses which perversely evaded divinely ordained restraints, he was obliged to emphasize the need for the formal submission through matrimony to divine laws. But, as a result of this formal submission, the ordinary principles of decency and modesty could regain the sanctions of the laws of God and absolute nature (pp. 60-61): relative natural laws could be converted into absolute ones. Defoe, then, believed that the brutal passions could become constructive qualities of life as long as reasonable men summoned relative natural laws in a way that celebrated the priority of divine law.

That Defoe refused to accept the plea of necessity as an extenuating circumstance in cases of sexual misdemeanour (p. 199), and that he regarded attempts to justify indecency as the work of the devil (p. 266), further show his religious perspective on natural law and his sense of the merely relative significance of natural impulses. Although his avowed purpose in writing *Conjugal Lewdness* was to encourage people to confess their sexual sins, Defoe's belief in religious morality made him discontented with limiting himself to satirical and expository modes. Hence, frequently he addresses himself in a monologue which laments contemporary mores: in recalling the limited scope of his own commentary he does not achieve a neutral tone. Rather, the tone impels the reader to recognize the writer's implicit religious values. When, for example, he concedes that 'I come therefore to search the Crime, and fully to expose it. Your Reason, and, if you have any, your Religion, will instruct you to reform it' (pp. 267-68), his mood is melancholic and his tone, varying between the impersonal and personal, is insulting and almost defiant: his words certainly betoken the firmness of his religious perspective on natural law. In a situation in which he pretends to remind himself that 'I must not Preach' he makes his judgment about the necessary religious mortification of the flesh inescapable.

Similar tensions to the ones that exist between natural and divine law in Defoe's consideration of sexual morality obtain in his discussion of political mores. A note in his most important political poem, *Jure Divino*, reveals that he upheld divine law as the ultimate imperative in political theory.

> It is a Universal Rule, that all Humane Laws are subject to the Divine; and if a Law is made by Humane Power, which contradicts the Laws of God, it is void in its Nature; and the Scripture gives a stated Rule for it in those Words, *Whether it be lawful to obey God rather than Man? Judge ye*; and the Practice of all Christian Ages agree to it.[2]

For Defoe, divine law was the final test of civil law. But his ideas about government, especially his belief in the legitimacy of resistance to political oppression, made him realize that natural law must also be used to sanction political theory and civil law.

> The Conjunction of the Faculties in resisting oppressive Authority, is no small Indication that it is a natural Principle, and if it be so, no Laws of Men can be said justly to contradict the Laws of Nature.[3]

Defoe clearly thought it conceivable for human nature to possess an integral spontaneity in reaction against political wrongs. But his awareness of political debate made him cautious about promoting natural law in relation to government. An opponent of the Catholic doctrine of the divine right of kings, he would not attack absolute monarchy with political rights in a secular way. While he held that the supporters of patriarchal theory abused religious argument, Defoe was alert to the moral dangers entailed by describing government either independently of religion or with thorough-going rationalism. Indeed, he preferred to consider politics from a biblical perspective: 'the Scripture is to be regarded in this Dispute above all other Testimonies.'[4] Defoe's religious sense of political theory caused him to differ both from the upholders of absolute monarchy and from the proposers of social contract, for, in his view, their argument over the relative importance of dominion and property ignored the perspective of *Genesis*. Agreeing with the absolutists that God had given man dominion over all the earth, Defoe denied their conclusion that this entailed the deputation of the 'Power of Government' from God to man. Again, Defoe accepted that the gift of property which God had endowed upon mankind and the freeholder's right to convey his dominion over property were indisputable.

But he rejected the absolutist contention that God gave to Adam a particular grant of the whole world. Instead, he held that 'Priority of Possession' was the only grounds for owning property, since individuals had equal rights to claim dominion in the world. He used biblical evidence, then, to support the view that possession of property is the source of political rights and, consequently, that property is prior to dominion. His purpose was to show that the original grant by God to man constituted a general right of property and that this right was insufficient to establish patriarchal absolutism. But, while Defoe refused to see government in terms of a religious covenant, he would not regard it as a social contract. For he held the source of government to lie in the perception of rational and spiritual truth and to be a matter of following natural law from a sense of religious identity.

> Government is an Appendix of Nature, one of the first rational Dictates to Man from his Understanding; 'tis form'd in the Soul, and therefore of Divine Original; he would cease to be rational, when he ceased to live regularly.

In Defoe's creed, each man saw by the 'Light of Nature' that his material and spiritual needs could be met only through recognizing the social requirement for government. Revealingly, Defoe defined government as nature directing man how to live as a reasonable creature. He explained this definition by insisting that God had so created the soul that it could depend on natural law, as distinct from divine dictates, for a political sense. But debate about the source and nature of political institutions was not as important to Defoe as recognizing man's innate capacity for government. In its most significant sense, government was a principle infused into man with life itself. Although, then, he is clear that particular institutions will be brought into being by natural law, Defoe's political theory, in that it is based upon religious conceptions of the soul and the creation, rests upon divine law.

In *Jure Divino* Defoe attempted to defend the constitutional changes which the Revolution of 1688 effected by supporting the proposition that a people has the right to check and to control its political constitution on the grounds of natural and divine law. But, if his main task was to vindicate the Revolution settlement against those who would not swear allegiance to the throne, namely, the high-church partisans who, from respect for the memory of James II, promoted both absolute monarchy and passive obedience, Defoe did not align himself with radical political theory despite his appreciation of radical thinkers.[5] He relied upon arguments from natural law for local effects, but he was not intent on devising a systematic explanation of government. For instance, he provides various accounts of the origin of political constitution.

At one time and another this is explained by the moral tyranny original sin imposed on mankind, by collective, rational reaction to the state of war which came about after the patriarchs could exercise sway no longer, by the individual's fundamental instincts for survival, by the individual's rational understanding of self-preservation and of the principles endowed upon man by nature, and by the religious sense of property which God instilled into man at the creation. Defoe is not concerned to relate and to order these causes of government. Rather, he exploits each for an immediate rhetorical effect. In general, the pragmatic and natural explanations of government allowed him to deflate transcendent theories of politics and to emphasize that man must be self-determining and self-reliant in his political life, while the rational and religious motifs permitted him to champion the worth of political stability and tradition as a way of avoiding merely secular accounts of politics and of warning that harmful social consequences, such as anarchy, derive from wholly natural explanations of politics.

Defoe's use of the word 'reason' in *Jure Divino* is a good indication of his preference to deal with natural and divine law in a rhetorical as distinct from systematic way. In the dedication to the poem he calls reason the first monarch of the world and the hereditary director of mankind. He also denominates reason as the guide of the passions and as the image of the Creator in the soul. The multivalence of reason, the fact that it can signify the faculty of judgment, the religious conscience, and the ideal of monarchy, reveals Defoe's deliberate refusal to produce a single-mindedly rational account of politics. Moreover, the regal imagery with which he depicts reason is obviously a technique for the displacement of absolutist ideas. Yet he compounds the regal imagery with allusions to the divine nature. Not only is reason a sacred, universal, and absolute principle which, in commanding obedience from mankind, is the only possible surrogate for the divine will on earth but also it possesses theological paradoxes. For example, it is transcendent because of its 'Uncontroul'd Sovereignty' and immanent because men do it "voluntary Homage." Defoe even fuses political and religious imagery. Hence, reason's 'Power is wholly Despotick' yet it is 'far from being a Tyrant.' The imagery with which Defoe depicts reason emphasizes its divine nature as well as suggesting that it is the only conceivable form of absolutism. It is the imagery which undermines the theory of the divine right of kings and which resists rationalistic political thought.

Neither is the other main account of reason in the poem systematic.[6] Defoe begins by complaining that too many people ignore its 'mighty Dictates.' Irritated by people's unwillingness to be politically self determining, he mocks the religiosity of those who '*Lift up the Hands* they should Employ *below.*' By insisting that '*Reason's the Sovereign Guide of Humane Things / ... The Soul of Sense, and Optick of the Mind,*' he argues that it is an integrating force which allows the individual to make sound judgments about worldly matters. Clearly, Defoe wishes to assert that reason is a sufficient imperative for the regulation of political life. But he is not content to leave the status of reason thus. For persuasive and moral motives he dignifies it by emphasizing its religious characteristics and functions. Hence, reason is '*The Light of Heaven,*' '*The very Life and Substance of the Man,*' and '*The Great Reflection of the Heavenly Ray.*' Because it is also '*The Heavenly Image in the Minds of Men,*' reason is necessarily '*The Great Corrector of the wandring Brain.*' Reason is at once equivalent to divine inspiration, the soul, and the conscience. It is thereby detached from notions of intellectual effort and logical abstraction. Despite his scorn for religiosity in situations demanding political action, Defoe claims that reason qualifies man for heaven, since it constitutes the perception of 'Light Divine' which elevates the soul to spiritual rapture. Having defined reason initially in terms of natural law to persuade people to political self-determination, Defore refuses to circumscribe his sense of reason within the political argument. That, for persuasive and moral causes, he cannot ignore the religious aspects of reason shows his tendency to let divine law dominate natural law.

Instead of developing a systematic argument, Defoe prefers to establish tensions between contrary assumptions and definitions. For example, at different times he claims both that the instinct of self-preservation can serve as a substitute for reason and that reason must oblige the individual to realize that the instinct of self-preservation possesses the status of a natural law. At one moment the reader is told to trust his nature implicitly but at the next he is enjoined to be analytical and self-conscious: reason should and should not be displaced, but these opposing injunctions are not explained in terms of one another. Again, at one time reason is the 'Soul of Sense,' that is, the animating centre of sense perception, whereas at the next its determination of the rules of providence depends on its being free from the mists of sense: reason makes the senses accurate but the senses make reason inaccurate. Similarly, Defoe explains in the introduction to *Jure Divino* that original sin has devastated the function of reason but then urges the individual not to abandon reason by failing to appreciate the divine grant of political liberty. In this contrary, Defoe at first reduces the function of reason to suggest, against the absolutists' notions, that the desire for political power is typical, ignoble, and irrational, whereas secondly he maintains, for the same purpose of denigrating passive obedience before arbitrary government, that a lack of rational commitment to politics aggravates original sin. His polemical desire to score rhetorical points ensures that he gives no single definition of reason and that he applies it in contrary ways.

The same is true of his use of natural law in *Jure Divino*. He finds natural law evident in a considerable variety of phenomena. He traces it in events and their consequences, in the relation of causes and effects, in the involuntary duty of self-preservation, in rational self-interest, in the dictates that arise from the structure of the mind, and in the rules of providence. Natural law is thus determinable by very different assumptions and analytical stances. However, Defoe makes no attempt to be discursive about the sources of natural law. Nor does he avoid contraries in his poetical exposition. Hence, it is not easy to connect his trust that society automatically regulates itself to his sense of the inevitability of the state of war. On account of his constant rhetorical hyperbole he emphasizes single aspects of natural law without developing them into a systematic concept. For instance, in the introduction he stresses that human nature so loves sin that grace is without effect, while later he affirms the orthodox view that grace can free man from the consequences of original sin. For reasons of persuasion, Defoe considered it to be a natural law for man to be both irremediably and remediably vicious: in the first case he depreciated political continuity in the past and in the second case he promoted a political tradition for the future. Consequently, when Defoe says that rights by power dominated natural rights in the state of nature his object is to emphasize the pragmatic, utilitarian characteristics of political contracts, yet when he avers that natural rights were more effective than rights by power his goal is to celebrate the agency of God in provoking man to political awareness. Defoe's commitment to moral exhortation obliged him to treat natural law in a contrary way: by maintaining that man is and is not independent of divine agency in political affairs, Defoe is enabled to be suggestive rather than dogmatic, provocative rather than doctrinaire.

The ambivalence with which he presents reason and natural law also applies to his treatment of political rights. He constantly argues that responsiveness to natural law is bound to result in constitutional laws which automatically win divine sanction, but he does not hold simply that political rights are justified directly by natural law and only indirectly so by divine law. Intent on arousing his readers from moral inertia by claiming that property and security became political rights only as a consequence of the Fall, Defoe also insists that such rights were entailed by creation, being the '*primo-genial* Off-spring of the Earth,' that man has a covenant with God to use his life and freedom properly, and that part of his property consists of the hope of heavenly reward. These insistences reveal Defoe's refusal to account for political rights independently of immediate divine sanction. His concession that natural law guides men to permissible and desirable political action is conditional upon divine law.

Defoe's unwillingness to apply natural law to politics in a straightforwardly positive way is evidenced by his eagerness to have liberty of conscience and freedom of worship considered as natural rights. Unlike Locke who equated natural and political rights and whose idea of toleration was a corollary to his belief in a rational constitution, Defoe possessed a religious sense which prevented him from treating natural and political rights equivalently. For Defoe, therefore, the political persecution of an individual for the sake of his conscience was a deprivation of his religious self-preservation and, as such, constituted an assault on his natural, as distinct from political, rights. Relying on natural law to invalidate the legislation which obliged Dissenters to conform with the Church of England, Defoe claims that it is a natural right for the individual's worship to be a free expression of his faith and thereby comes close to equating natural and religious rights.[7]

Defoe's religious sense underlies his awareness that simple talk of natural rights risks the danger of anarchy and causes him to promote the interdependence of natural duties and natural rights. Hence, he uses natural law to emphasize the right of government to exact natural duties from citizens. He thought the best way of institutionalizing the state's natural right to exert absolute moral restraint on its people was to establish an oath of allegiance and fidelity. By performing such a declaration the people would be aroused to the 'Natural Obligations that lie upon them to submit to the Government.' If, because natural duties and rights are reciprocal, natural law justified a government's enforcement of a religious oath, it was obvious to Defoe that, since an oath was an act of faith and an acknowledgement of the divine nature, the stability of government depended directly on respect for divine law. Although natural law regulated rights and duties, Defoe thought it inevitable that for the state to possess the proper relation of rights and duties divine law had to regulate natural law.

Defoe's carefulness not to equate natural and political rights and his view that natural law must draw upon divine law if the state is to operate morally with natural rights and duties provide more evidence that religious sense and revelation are integral to his discussion of political mores. In this respect it is interesting to note that very similar imagery to that with which Defoe dignified reason in the dedication to *Jure Divino* is used to describe peace in *A Hymn to Peace*. For instance, peace is described as the regulator of the passions, as 'Emblem of the Sacred Rest,' and as the state of grace: ''Tis bright Essential Happiness, / Because He dwells within, whose Name is PEACE.' Besides defining peace as revelation and emphasizing its priority to reason,

Defoe claims that it is the foundation of property and social existence. He also insists that only if society is informed by revelation will it be able to appeal to natural law legitimately in political matters.[9] That, for Defoe, religion provides the ultimate, positive standard for politics is also evident in his statement that the Scriptures 'prescribe no Obedience of the Subject contrary to the Laws of Nature, the Laws of Nations, or the particular Laws of our own Country.'[10]

In his attempts to reform social attitudes and particularly in his efforts to encourage people to be more compassionate towards their less fortunate fellows, Defoe perhaps manifests his most concerted application of natural law.[11] Yet when in *Serious Reflections* he urges the plight of debtors and of others whose reduced circumstances render them susceptible to public condemnation, his references to natural rights are delimited by religious assumptions and definitions with the result that his use of natural law cannot be described as systematic. Indeed, his allusions to necessity, the natural dictate of self-preservation, are sufficiently ambivalent to demonstrate that, far from intending to suggest that natural law provides new and positive standards for social behaviour, he articulates natural principles mostly for the rhetorical purpose of arousing people to regard civil law from the perspective of religious conscience. On the one hand, he presents necessity as if it is irresistible, but his point of view is not a naturalistic one.

> Necessity is above the Power of human Nature; and for Providence to suffer a Man to fall into that Necessity, is to suffer him to sin; because Nature is not furnish'd with Power to defend itself, nor is Grace itself able to fortify the Mind against it. (p. 39)

On the other hand, he emphasizes that necessity can and must be resisted, and he defines the moral effort requisite to do so in religious rather than natural terms.

> To be honest, when Circumstances grow narrow, Relations turbulent and quarrelsome, when Poverty stares at us, and the World threatens; this Blessing is from Heaven, and can only be supported from thence. God Almighty is very little beholding to them, who will serve him just as long as he feeds them. (p. 42)

The rhetorical contexts of these two statements about necessity are very different. In the first Defoe addresses his readers as if they are likely condemners of those who have committed crimes from necessity, while in the second he assumes that his audience possesses the inclination to rationalize its own crimes. In the first passage, then, in order to deflate complacent judgment, Defoe insists upon the power of necessity: he suggests that, since no human or religious resources can withstand providence and since necessity is an agent of providence, the sole moral response of the Christian towards a fellow who is subject to necessity is compassion. In the second passage he promotes moral resilience by maintaining that necessity never allows the individual to relax his efforts to be religious and that, because the individual's closeness to God is the effect of grace, it must always be a matter for deeper spiritual gratitude rather than for shallow self-congratulation. While these passages reveal Defoe's contrary treatment of both necessity and grace, they are complementary on account of their religious assumptions. By advancing the conclusions that, if grace cannot overcome necessity, providence allows necessity to predominate and that, if grace conquers necessity, Heaven is the agent of victory, he makes the religious purposes of his consideration of natural law inescapably clear.

In setting out to change the harsh way in which people judge their neighbours by providing insight into the nature of honesty, Defoe pretends to be untheoretical and secular, rather than philosophical and religious, in stance. This profession of attitude, however, is more rhetorical than categorical since his discussion of honesty contains many more references to the laws of conscience than to natural law. For example, despite the secular imagery in the expression that 'Heaven's *Chancery*' in every man's breast will condemn him as 'a Rebel to Nature and his own Conscience' if he regulates his conduct towards his fellows only by civil war, it is clear that in Defoe's mind natural standards are subordinate to religious ones. He actually belittles the dictates of custom and nature since they can only say of the man who limits himself to the letter of the law in his dealings with neighbours that he is hard-hearted and inhuman, whereas he champions the dictates of conscience because they inform men that charity is a religious duty which must be discharged on account of the unacceptable gap between 'the Politicks of the Nation' and the 'Laws of God.'[12] When he does use natural law to persuade people to a new sense of honesty, he usually bases his argument on biblical episodes. Hence, he adopts and expatiates upon Solomon's statement that a poor man who steals to satisfy hunger deserves compassion rather than condemnation.[13] More interestingly, he retells the story of King David which Christ relates to the Pharisees after they chide the disciples for plucking ears of corn on the sabbath. Defoe maintains that, since David broke the commandment not to eat the shew-bread out of respect for the natural law of his hunger, his character was not destroyed by that single, illicit act. But, whereas Christ's account is support for His claim that His authority frees the disciples from observance of the law of the temple, Defoe, somewhat extremely, generalizes the implications of Christ's argument and states that Christ's story declares that necessity makes unlawful things lawful.[14] Although Defoe changes the force of the biblical story by underemphasizing the significance of Christ's authority, he still relies heavily upon general biblical authority to support the contention that the satisfaction of hunger is a law of nature. Furthermore, even if in this instance he is prepared to consider that natural law may counteract a divine commandment, he usually gives natural law a much more restricted function. For, in arguing that an individual may commit an ultimate crime without necessarily deserving either divine or human condemnation, he does not really aver that necessity justifies crime. At times he may seem to do so as a rhetorical strategy for disturbing complacency, but consistently he proposes that necessity makes unlawful things lawful neither in themselves nor in their circumstances. Consequently, he affirms that 'The Guilt of a Crime with respect to its being a Crime, *viz.* an Offence against God, is not removed by the Circumstances of Necessity.'[15] Rather, these circumstances 'make the Reason, Why we that have fallen, should rather be pity'd than reproach'd by those who think they stand.' The point is that Defoe prefers to explain necessity in religious terms. For him it is a necessary and religious condition of life that the righteous man falls seven times a day, and, since it is inevitable that at one time or another all men prove themselves knaves from the divine viewpoint because of their vulnerability to necessity, it is the duty of him who happens to be untouched by necessity to be grateful to the protection of providence instead of blaming others for succumbing to circumstances. In Defoe's judgment, the man who pretended to know his fellow well enough to condemn him for a single lapse of honesty and to pursue him with the civil law was ignorant not only of the power of necessity but also, and more importantly, of divine law. For, by so exacerbating his fellow's necessity, the uncompassionate man was likely to harden his neighbour to his circumstances and to distance him from a religious sense of succumbing to necessity.

Defoe's religious conviction that an honest man could never employ necessity as an exculpating or extenuating plea explains why he did not think of himself as promoting natural morality when he proposed that men of conscience should not bring civil law to bear on necessitous people. The appreciation of divine disposition, which obliged him to regard an individual's opportunity to be compassionate as a 'particular Gift' from God, committed him to believing that, as soon as the honest man escaped necessity, he would be the first to reprove himself, repent, and make restitution. Although he announced that 'Necessity makes an honest Man a Knave' as a rhetorical means of startling those people who possessed a merely conventional sense of honesty, Defoe did not hold that a really honest man, that is, a man with a religious awareness of his own character and conduct, could be made into a knave by necessity.[16] As far as Defoe was concerned, the honest victim of necessity

> never fails to express his own Dislike of it; he acknowledges upon all Occasions, both to God and to Man, his having been overcome, and been prevail'd upon to do, what he does not approve of; he is too much asham'd of his own Infirmity, to pretend to vindicate the Action, and he certainly is restor'd to the first regulation of his Principles, as soon as the Temptation is over. (p. 45)

To Defoe it was inconceivable that an honest person would rationalize the conduct to which he might be forced by necessity and that he would continue to behave outside the condition of necessity according to the natural standards that allowed him to preserve himself in that condition. In order to avoid seeming to support these possibilities, Defoe stresses natural law's potential for changing the attitudes of people towards their lapsed fellows: he describes necessity in order to alert people to the general vulnerability to circumstance and not in order to provide a set of natural standards which motivate or legitimate conduct. He held that, to the extent to which necessity was a natural law, it helped people to regard the secular conditions of life from a religious perspective and to realize that vulnerability to circumstance was an aspect of original sin.

> But when we are considering human Nature subjected by the Consequences of *Adam*'s Transgression, to Frailty and Infirmity; and regarding things from Man to Man, the Exigencies and Extremities of streightned Circumstances seem to me to be the most prevailing Arguments, why the Denomination of a Man's general Character ought not, *by his fellow Mortals (subject to the same Infirmities)* to be gathered from his Mistakes, his Errors or Failings, no not from his being guilty of any extraordinary Sin, but from the Manner and Method of his Behaviour. (p. 46)

By subsuming necessity to the Fall and by suggesting that character be judged in terms of what amounts to spiritual biography, Defoe can be seen to place his call for compassion towards necessitous individuals under the class of divine law with the consequences that natural law seems limited to providing society with a sense of its natural duties rather than giving the individual an awareness of his natural rights. He insisted that society acknowledge its natural and religious duties because he believed that by promoting honesty it would compensate for natural depravity. Hence, he urged that the sense of honesty which natural law might help society to realize is ultimately religious:

> So far as it is found upon Earth, so much of the first Rectitude of Nature, and of the Image of God, seems to be restor'd to Mankind. (p. 31)

For Defoe, a society which employs natural law to define its duties is one which, by definition, restores creation in the most ideal of ways.

This conclusion should make it clear that Defoe did not conceive of natural and divine law as two equally valid but separate moral systems and that he treated them neither separately nor systematically. Far from believing that divine law confused natural law, he judged the latter of value only as it was related to or justified by the former.[17] By stressing the religious meaning of natural laws he was enabled to argue that natural laws increase the effectiveness of religious ethics in day-to-day life. While, then, he did employ natural law as an instrument of social satire and with an eager awareness of rhetorical strategy, he also used it to extend traditional religious values into sexual, political, and social mores. Indeed, the most positive function Defoe gives to natural law is its relation to divine law. When he makes statements about natural law, frequently he restates religious truths without appearing to do so. Often, too, natural law becomes a medium for sacramental meaning. Hence the rhetorical ambivalence with which he treats reason, natural law, natural rights, and necessity reveals his commitment to a flexible didacticism and shows that he sought continuously for new ways to celebrate his divine perspective even as he promoted social reform and earthly happiness.

CHAPTER 3

The Revolution of 1688

> The present State of the Nation may most perfectly and clearly be understood without any search into Antiquity, other than by looking back to the *Late Revolution:* The *Errors* of *Past Reigns,* the *Rancour* of *Civil-War,* the *Fury* of the *Restoration,* the Intrigues of King *Charles* II and the *Jehu Drivings* of King *James* II all had their Periods here.¹

Defoe was an eager apologist for the Revolution of 1688 because to him it represented a fresh start for life in England. He saw the Revolution as providing a break from the past and a not-to-be-missed opportunity of structuring life more morally than previously. Certainly, the Revolution provoked Defoe to consider society in connected and integrated ways. His writings during William III's reign suggest interesting notions about the relation of the state and morality. Sooner or later in these immediately post-Revolution works, his explorations of constitutional and political subjects involve religious ideas. For in these writings his main purposes are to celebrate the Revolution as a sign of God's concern for England and to berate those who failed to realize that their religious duty obliged them to appreciate and strengthen the state. He held that, although the Revolution had effected important constitutional changes, more refined attitudes and ways of thinking were necessary in order for the constitution to inform daily life properly. Hence, he himself was keen to publicize the relevance of the constitution to social reform.²

There can be no doubt that Defoe was moved personally and deeply by the Revolution and that it possessed a symbolic force in his mind. Consequently, nineteen years afterwards he could look back with a strong sense of devotion to November 4, 1688. To him it was

> A Day dedicate to great Actions, and sacred in all the Undertakings, I shall ever set my Hand to, or all the Works I shall go about.³

But the day the Prince of Orange landed on English soil was endued in his memory with a general religious significance too, since providence had ordained that day for the nation's spiritual relief. More than merely a political event, William's arrival had disburdened English pilgrims and made the prospect of the promised land clearer. On that day 'the Lord brought us out of the House of Bondage, ... a Bondage of Soul-Tyranny as well as Body-Servitude.' His analogy to the Israelites reveals that the symbolic significance of the Revolution to Defoe was public as well as private. While, then, he was personally dedicated to honouring the memory of William and Mary, in emphasizing their inspiration of social reform he sought to explain why, as instruments of the Revolution, the King and Queen ought to be revered in the public mind.

> The late Queen *Mary*, of heavenly Memory, for her Piety and blessed Example, appear'd in her Time gallantly in the Cause of Virtue; Magistrates were encourag'd to punish Vice, new Laws made to restrain it, and Justice seem'd to be at Work to reclaim it.[4]

His personal appreciation of the monarchs' efforts to reform society is translated, especially in the works which he composed during William's reign, into an attempt to heighten public awareness of the ethical and spiritual implications of the Revolution.

The symbolic significance of the Revolution led Defoe to argue on behalf of the new constitution and the Bill of Rights in a heightened way. In his mind, support of the Revolution involved more than political principle: it entailed general understanding and spiritual gratitude.

> I must needs think it no undue Censure to say, that no Man, who understands the Constitution of this *Monarchy*, can be against the *present Government* out of *principle;* for whoever questions the right of it, either has not used due means of informing himself, how fully the settlement is warranted by the Constitution; or has that want of Judgement, which makes him a dependent upon the Judgement of others.[5]

To suggest the redundancy of theoretical opposition to the Revolution and to defend William's administration against the Jacobite non-jurors Defoe claims that a proper understanding of the constitution assures judgment in its favour and that this positive reaction to the constitution is beyond the scope of political debate. Certainly, he felt that those who opposed the Revolution manifested a lamentable sense of political tradition, but he placed greater emphasis on the fact that, since they did not recognize the Revolution as 'the Lord's doing,' they revealed religious perversity. Their intransigence prompted him to employ biblical typology to express his fears for the nation's spiritual welfare. That the nation was not of one mind about the Revolution betokened that 'like the Children of *Israel* in the Wilderness, instead of going on to possess that *Canaan* God seems to have design'd for us, we are for making a Captain to return again in to Egypt; and to put our necks into that Yoke, which neither we nor our Fathers were able to bear.'⁶ From Defoe's viewpoint, the supporters of James II, in denying allegiance to William and the constitution, were attempting not only to enslave England to France but also to ignore the biblical precedent that was established when God caused the Israelites to rebel against Pharoah. Defoe criticized the Jacobites for lacking the religious sense requisite to political discrimination: in his eyes they were stupid enough to hate all rebellion on account of the Civil War and to 'despise and destroy their own Rights and Liberties, because they were asserted by a Company of Rebels so long ago.' For Defoe the great difference between the Civil War and the Revolution was that in 1688 there had been 'a Call from Heaven it self' which, since it was as immediate and powerful as the one which converted St. Paul, reflected adversely upon the Jacobites' spiritual responsiveness.

Defoe himself revered the Revolution settlement because of his religious sense of abstract political ideas: he thought that the new structure of ideal relations in government afforded society the prospect of increased stability and security. He could be enthusiastic about the constitution on the grounds of its moral effectiveness.

> Here the Populace have liberty without a Democratical Confusion and Fury; the Nobility have all the priviledges to which Aristocracy itself could intitle them, without the necessity of running into Factions and Cabals for it; and the King's Power so equally ballanced between the Two other, that his Power can hardly ever degenerate into tyranny, nor, on the other side, while he governs by Law, can he ever want Authority either to protect or correct his Subjects, or means to reward Vertue, or discourage Vice, which are the great Ends for which Civil Government was at first instituted.⁷

The mixed constitution and its balance of power seemed to guarantee moral reformation on account of religious models. That the three major elements of the constitution, the King, the Lords, and the Commons, were equally necessary to the making and abrogating of laws was all the more pleasing because it was analogous to the Trinity. Moreover, while the fact that the King's executive power was now restricted by the judicial and legislative systems pleased Defoe's sense of political theory because such a restriction gave implicit acknowledgment to the original power of the people, namely, their inherent right to delegate authority to kings, he was more gratified that the contractual nature of the new constitution could be paralleled to God's covenant with mankind. Since the Creator had limited his power by undertaking a contract with man, it was morally inevitable for the people and their kings to model their relationship on the divine paradigm and to recognize the divine original of political contracts.

Of course, Defoe had rhetorical motives for adopting a religious attitude towards the constitution. By relating the Revolution settlement to ultimate value, he was enabled authoritatively both to persuade people to revere the constitution and to dissuade others from taking it too lightly. He was particularly aware that by vindicating natural political rights in his defence of the Revolution he might be seen as diminishing 'Public Authority.' Consequently, he explained that none of James II's crimes against individuals caused the King to forfeit his prerogative and that only his abuse of the constitution in his attempts to subject England to France and to develop the dispensing power was just grounds for his dismissal. In order to discourage an easy sense of rebellion Defoe maintained that it was preferable for the individual to suffer injustice than for the public peace to be disturbed without adequate cause. Indeed, he argued that the individual should endure an unjust sentence without thinking of his own rights, 'for although Justice be never so violated, yet if the Law be preserv'd intire, and the Constitution and Basis of the Government remain firm and unshaken, the Subject must be content to suffer, and neither Oppose nor Depose the King.'[8] This statement reveals his insistence that revolution cannot be related simply to individual rights and shows that he cited political rights in a rational and theoretical way because he applied them to notions of the public, rather than private, good. By limiting the applicability of political rights in this way Defoe hoped to obviate revolutionary clamours against William. Finally, however, Defoe uses biblical quotation to comment on unjustified discontent with William. He prays for William's success in government by citing a verse from St. Paul who had adapted it from Isaiah: the general tenor of the verse is that success in the prophetic tradition is always accompanied by contempt. In this verse Isaiah had prophesied that, despite abusive treatment, Christ's ministry would succeed and St. Paul had indicated that the suffering which he underwent as a preacher only added to the glory of God. Defoe places himself in this prophetic tradition.

> Therefore I . . . *beseech you that you receive not the Grace of God in vain*; for as God may truly say, *he has heard us in a time accepted, in the day of salvation he hath succour'd us*; so may I also, *Behold, now is the accepted time; Behold now is the day of salvation*. And let us all be *careful that we give no offence in any thing, that the Ministry be not blamed*. But that we may all with one Heart and Mouth bless God for his wonderful Deliverance, and pray for the Prosperity and long life of King *WILLIAM* and Queen *MARY*, whom God grant long to Reign. Amen.[9]

Here Defoe preaches that, since King William is an agent and messenger of divine grace, his administration should be esteemed as beyond reproach. In recommending that 'Public Authority' be viewed as a divine manifestation, Defoe's rhetoric argues for the relevance of religious deliberation in political matters, thereby displacing interest in natural rights.

By adopting a religious attitude to the Revolution settlement Defoe acquired rhetorical resources for the promotion of William's policies, especially his foreign policies. In *The Advantages of the Present Settlement* (1689), for example, he emphasizes the controlling part which providence played in the Revolution. He compares this political deliverance to deliverance from the plague because 'the means used to effect this Design, being so unproportionate to this great end designed, makes the success a Prodigy.' (p. 24). Since providence had established William on the throne so extraordinarily, his policies possessed the highest imperatives, and the English were obliged religiously to support the Protestant alliances in Europe to which William had pledged himself. In Defoe's argument, support of William's foreign policy is a political duty which is indistinguishable from obedience to a religious commandment. Another example of his disposition of religious persuasiveness in political matters is seen in his argument that integral to foreign policy is the King's ability to maintain an army in peace because such an army is essential to the balance of power in Europe. To Defoe there was a degree of irreligion in those Tories who would not realize the extent to which the political situation in Europe affected England's commerce and colonies and who spoke in favour of self-sufficiency and insularity. Although he contended that a standing army was wholly consistent with the Bill of Rights, his ultimate support of a standing army is a statement of political faith which contains an analogy to religious testimony.

> I am as positively assur'd of the Safety of our Liberties under the Conduct of King and Parliament, while they concur, *as I am of the Salvation of Believers by the Passion of our Saviour.*[10]

For Defoe it was an item of faith that, given the constitutional restrictions on military expenditure, there could be no reasonable objection to a standing army. Hence, he condemned the opponents of William's military policy who cried up despotic power as unorthodox in political and religious creed. That the King's opponents were prejudiced by Commonwealth and Socinian doctrines was reason enough why William deserved the support of orthodox Christians.

As the problems associated with succession to the Spanish throne became more acute, thereby making William's foreign policy seem more sound, Defoe tried to disarm what he perceived to be increasing resistance to military involvement in Europe by repeatedly emphasizing the need to protect the Protestant alliance against Catholic imperialism through preparation for a religious war with France.[11] He tried to show that inaction would endanger the structure of English life by undermining industrial manufactures, employment, merchant shipping, and the money supply. To allay hostility to William's policies further, he argued that they were consistent with the Bill of Rights, and he insisted that the moral restructuring of society which the Revolution settlement prompted could not be effected without a commitment to foreign policy. Defoe's opposition to secular politics and the developing party system is also revealed by his defence of the King's right to sign the treaties of partition: he was adamant that the Revolution had not stripped monarchs of the traditional prerogative of making leagues in their own name.[12] To overcome factionalism and to demonstrate the feasibility of a national political attitude Defoe equated rational self-interest with religious duty and maintained that William's role and policies, because of their importance to the constitution and to daily life, deserved uniform religious respect.

> *The Liberties of this Nation, the Property of the Subject, the Encrease of Manufactures, and the Maintenance of the Poor, are Things worthy of Debates in the Great Council of the Nation, the* Parliament. *But these are all Antecedent to the Great Relative* Religion; *These are all but Circumstances to the Great Essential, Circles drawn about the Great Center* Religion.[13]

For Defoe the gap between political consciousness and religious conscience had to be closed. As long as people did not have the Protestant religion next to their hearts, their 'Politick Interest,' that is, their political understanding of the need for leagues and alliances, was inconsequential as far as he was concerned. That political factions existed which in one extreme 'would advance the Prerogative of Kings to the Ruin of the Subjects Properties' and in another wanted to reduce 'the Just Power of the King to the Will and Pleasure of a Party' showed to Defoe that there was no prevailing sense of the constitution and society as 'the City of our God.'[14] He claimed that to permit the prejudices of extreme political ideas to interfere with the nation's Protestant duty to Europe entailed that 'our Saviour shou'd rank us among them, who *when he was hungry, gave him no meat*; or, when he was in Distress, gave him no help.'[15] Defoe insisted, then, that 'Politick Interest' too often caused moral evasiveness. For instance, he felt convinced that people who pretended concern for personal liberty in the debate about a standing army overvalued their individual freedom because they ignored the religious nature of the public good. He found such individuals not just socially intolerable: he thought them as irreligious as the lukewarm Laodiceans. Their self-interested evasion of the need for Protestant commitment in Europe rendered them enemies of God. Against the consequences of mere political interest Defoe urged the priority of religious sense:

> Defend Religion and Politick Interests will be easily secured; *a jove Principium, God and your Country*; but first God, and then your Country.[16]

Indeed, without a feeling for the priority of religion in their hearts the people would encounter grave political consequences, for God 'made our Liberty so dependent on, and relative to our Religion, that it is morally impossible Liberty in *England* can be any longer liv'd then Religion.' From Defoe's point of view, religion did not simply provide the ultimate justification for William's foreign policies: it also explained the value of national constitutions and international regulations to the moral life.

His own religious sense of the Revolution was responsible for Defoe's being inventive both in the promotion and in the devising of policy. He was not content simply to promulgate conventional ideas: his ability as a projector allowed him to see the relation of national and international issues in provocative ways. When, for instance, he was angered by news of the persecution of French Protestants, he did not claim that war should be declared against France, even though he realized that this persecution constituted a violation of one of the clauses of the Treaty of Ryswick. Showing restraint, he pointed out that there could be no justification of military intervention on behalf of the Huguenots. With a moral view of the relativity of natural law, he maintained that the Huguenots' 'Natural Right' to peace and prosperity derived from the French constitution and that, while natural law permitted them to apply force to protect themselves and to change the constitution, it would not justify interference from England.[17] But he was conservative in stressing the constitutional limitations to natural law in order to be radical in his consideration of it in international relations. For the purpose, then, of legitimating the state's indirect intervention into French affairs, he summoned the law of retaliation which, while normally considered a natural law available only to individuals, he extended to be applicable to 'Collective Bodies.' In his mind this conversion of an individual to a national right was sanctioned by divine justice and the concept of ultimate reward and punishment. By means of this law of retaliation Defoe felt justified in warning France to stop the persecution of Protestants: he suggested that Protestant countries should persecute and expel Catholics at the same time as welcoming Protestant refugees. As a projector, Defoe gave this threat of retaliation an added deterrent in the shape of an ingenious economic argument. He insisted that, whereas Protestant countries with their advanced industrial economies would benefit from an influx of refugees because of the concomitant increase in consumer demand and in efficient use of resources, Catholic countries with their relatively backward economies could not tolerate the arrival of large numbers of poor refugees. This argument betokens Defoe's expectations about the ability of William's foreign policy to effect change in the world and, at the same time, to further English interests: as a rhetorical proposal it reflects his estimation of the Protestant alliance's exercise of moral suasion and as innovative policy it reveals his desire to convince the English that implementation of international strategies can but safeguard domestic advantages.

Defoe's awareness of the reciprocity of international and national interests led him to be quite radical in his projects for defending the significance of the Revolution. For example, in *The Succession to the Crown of England, Consider'd* (1701), after beginning by proposing that an enquiry be opened to examine the legitimacy of the Duke of Monmouth, he ends with the more obviously revolutionary notion that the crown be given to the heirs of Monmouth without any enquiry.[18] Perhaps this proposal is not outrageous considering that it was made just after the last of Anne's seventeen children had died and before the Act of Settlement which gave the succession after Anne to the House of Hanover had been drawn up. But Defoe's desire to have an heir to William whose strength would afford national stability and international power, together with his criticism of Anne and the Elector of Hanover as potential monarchs, is truly revolutionary in the sense that he puts much greater emphasis on the principles of the Revolution settlement than he does upon tradition and lineage. His suggestion that the crown be given to the Earl of Dalkeith who, in addition to being Monmouth's son, was a Scot was motivated by Defoe's realization that the Scots needed to be placated for the failure of their colony at Darien. He believed that, if they were not mollified, it would be necessary for England to keep troops close to the border with Scotland. This possibility he regarded as an irresponsible reduction of military commitment to Europe. His proposal to have Dalkeith appointed king is also explained by his concession to prejudice against foreigners, which is somewhat surprising given the fierce attack on chauvinism in *The True-Born Englishman* (1701). After acknowledging that William's problems with governing were aggravated by his being foreign, he maintains that the Hanoverians will do worse than William and suggests that, if the English people are allowed to elect a native king, their actual experience of Revolution principles will give them a sense of unity and nationality that will make them eager supporters of foreign policy. Although he believed that the military prowess of Dalkeith by contrast with the gouty, childless condition of Anne would endow the monarchy with a necessary appeal, his concession to prejudice serves to heighten his trust that the appeal of the process of the

Revolution settlement should be more important than that of an individual monarch because of the way in which it secures political commitment to national and international interests. To Defoe the possible invitation to Dalkeith constituted an opportunity to re-enact the Revolution.

On account of his eagerness to celebrate the Revolution by word and deed it is not surprising that, when some petitioners from Kent complained to Parliament in 1701 about its reluctance to support William's policies and had their spokesman detained and their petition vilified, he went to their defence by composing *Legion's Memorial* and delivering it to Parliament. In this fiercely revolutionary address, he took a righteous delight in chastising Tory and Jacobite members for failing to grant the King the Bills of Supply. Partly as a result of the hectoring style of this address, proceedings against the petitioners and four peers who were key supporters of William were dropped, and Parliament rushed through the approval of moneys before seeking the safety of prorogation.[19] In *Legion's Memorial* he presents himself as the spokesman for the freeholders of England in a very blunt and direct manner, and by asserting that it is their right to require and their power to compel he insists that the freeholders are the masters of their representatives. He even justifies the use of *'Extrajudicial'* methods to force Parliament to recognize these considerations.[20] The vehemence of his rhetoric on behalf of the political values of the Revolution settlement is matched by the rigour of the criticism that he applies to Members of Parliament for ignoring the reformation of manners. The members had betrayed the trust of God, King, and people because they were vicious in

> Morals and Religion; Lewd in Life, and Erroneous in Doctrine, having publick Blasphemers and Impudent Deniers of the Divinity of our Saviour among you, and suffering them unreproved and unpunished to the infinite Regret of all good Christians, and the just Abhorrence of the whole Nation.[21]

With such trenchant feelings about the integrity of religious and political values, Defoe became a relentless campaigner to have members who respected the Bill of Rights and the need to restructure society returned to the next Parliament.

Yet his confidence in the symbolic significance of the Revolution meant that he did not always assume an aggressive role in addressing his political adversaries. The death of James II, for example, gave him an opportunity to be conciliatory towards the Jacobites in England. In *The Present State of Jacobitism Considered* (1701) he moderately invites them to reconsider their attitude to the Revolution. By pointing out gently their mistaken attitudes towards international as well as national political circumstances he hopes to reconcile the Jacobites to their constitution. After acknowledging their limited civil rights, he argues that their interest is still to accept the Protestant constitution on the grounds that French support of their cause in England is not to be counted on. He maintains that such support is at best simply a strategy for Louis XIV to divert English troops from Europe. Another political reason why he affirms that the Jacobites should accept the Revolution settlement is that, in excluding James II's son from succession, the Bill of Rights had nullified all oaths of allegiance to the Stuart cause. He premises that an oath of allegiance requires constitutional force and proceeds to reduce their hopes for a Stuart restoration by demonstrating that their oath lacks this force. The final argument which he presents quietly to the Jacobites is based on his appreciation of providence's disposition of dates for monitory purposes. He sees such day-fatality in the facts that James II was voted to have abdicated on the same date as he ascended the throne and that he died on the anniversary of the Fire of London. His sure feeling about the integrity of political and religious circumstance enabled him to be steady in his attempt to comprehend the Jacobites fully into the Revolution settlement.

The firmness of his convictions about the Revolution enabled him, moreover, to develop subtle rhetorical strategies in which he could appeal to his political opponents in order to criticize them implicitly. Such a strategy unfolds in *Reasons against a War with France* (1701). This title, given its historical context, suggests that the viewpoint of the tract, insofar as it is opposed to military involvement, might be insular, that is, might correspond with Tory views. But the title serves an ironical function because it helps Defoe to delay his criticism of the Tories. By beginning, then, with a hostile commentary on the country's overhasty preparation for war Defoe does not mind appearing to fall in with Tory prejudice against the foreign policy necessitated by the Revolution. But this implicit appeal to a Tory audience is ironical: although his actual and eventual perspective is not that of the Tories, he leads them on. Particular evidence for this is found in his posturing criticism of the populace's outcry against Parliament's harsh treatment of the Kentish petitioners, a position opposite to his stance in *Legion's Memorial* and his other writings in support of the Revolution. His initial point, however, is that French aid for the Old Pretender is not a sufficient cause for declaring war on France and that the announcement of this so-called support is a French expedient to discountenance the English and to distract them from deliberate continental policy. He calls for the nation to ignore the insult and to realize that such aid is merely nominal. Since 'Natural antipathies are not just ground of a War between Nations' (p. 3), he refuses to support the war effort. He emphasizes that the nation should consider itself in a state of war only if the French break the treaties that were established to protect the balance of power in Europe. In this emphasis Defoe implicitly invites Tory readers to consider that the very prerogative that they denied to William, namely, the right to form leagues, is the single reason why at the moment war is not justified. Of course, through the irony of hinting that the Tories are right for the wrong reason, he makes it more obvious that there is a right reason for the justification of war. Defoe is clear that one can be waged only in the name of the Revolution settlement.

The works which Defoe composed during William's reign and which are not directly concerned with justifying and promoting the constitution and government policy nevertheless usually criticize aspects of public and private life and theorize about society from a political point of view. *An Essay upon Projects* (1697), for example, sets out to show how institutions, individuals, economic conduct, and manners must achieve moral renewal through the adoption of refined structures or regulations. But by basing his schemes for reformation upon increased state control and upon the individual's improved self-reliance he clearly assumes that greater social happiness will augment the effectiveness with which the Revolution settlement is administered. Hence, his project for tax reform since it recognizes with distaste that current legislation allows the rich to avoid paying taxes and burdens the poor with unduly heavy indirect taxation is informed with social justice and general welfare. But the ultimate reason for proposing a new system of direct taxation which measures income and assets is the provision of an efficient means for the administration to raise revenue for the implementation of foreign policy. Aware that, since the business community benefits from war more than the working poor, it should pay the major share of taxes, Defoe also knows that legislation alone will not oblige people to be socially responsible and to curb their economic individualism. Consequently, he suggests that a common cause is more effective than statutory force and that the authority of the state must depend on national pride. Although he does not cease emphasizing the need for greater state power, he realizes that the state will attain to this degree of power only if individuals so share the state's goals that by regulating their lives and affairs they give that power to the state which legislation by itself cannot obtain. Hence, he praises the Bank of England for contributing to the war effort by giving the state greater control over money and credit and by reducing the influence of goldsmiths, but he criticizes this financial institution because its low interest rates reveal that its managers are more interested in satisfying their own speculation than in establishing a true national circulation of funds. From his point of view the legislation founding the bank could not succeed in providing the state with power and control unless its managers and people in general believed in the connection of economic development and national security. So, in urging communities to improve transportation and communications he contends that not only will more people be employed and trade grow but also the greater circulation of money will strengthen the power of the state.

His concentration on schemes of self-help in *An Essay upon Projects* is an attempt to persuade people to form cooperatives partly in order that the national treasury might be relieved of certain domestic burdens. Indeed, in these projects for group insurance he maintains that national security depends upon the various sections of society regulating their lives and resources in order to protect themselves against their relative risks. He projects, for example, that, since a society for seamen will guarantee their income and welfare and allow them to be more conscientious in their dangerous duties, the national interest is bound to be served. He also claims that a society for widows would permit them to receive subsistence as a right rather than a charity as well as reducing public expenditure on hospitals. He even proposes coercing the poor into contributing towards their old age in order to maximize the revenue for the implementation of foreign policy. Although his proposals stress that the self-reliance of sections of society is necessary for a strong state, he does not let his political perspective overwhelm religious and humanitarian considerations. So, the imperative for joining friendly societies he finds in the 'Divine Rule' (p. 123) that men must be charitable to their fellows, and in his suggestion that authors levy a tax on their own revenue in order to donate to the care of the mentally ill he emphasizes society's obligation to charity. Of course, even this suggestion discriminates between the responsibilities of society and state. While, however, in most of his projects he was intent on discovering the social structure or form by which general attitudes could be reformed and the state could be left freer to pursue national policies, in some cases he argued that the state should institutionalize such attitudes by law. To a certain extent he thought it necessary for the state to remind its citizens by legislation to treat one another humanely. Certainly, he was disgusted by the materialistic callousness which contemporary legislation against debtors did nothing to discourage. He felt that the creditor's legal right to imprison the debtor was inhuman because the honest debtor was thereby rendered 'perfectly uncapable of any thing but *starving*' (p. 192) and ineffectual because dishonest debtors could easily retire with their assets to the sanctuaries of 'the *Mint* and *Friars*' and thus evade the law.[22] He believed that the state ought to rationalize its law. It could do this by abolishing the legal right to sanctuary and by founding a court of inquiry into bankruptcies which could differentiate between dishonest and honest debtors and help the latter to begin again in business free from the excessive claims of creditors. Needless to say, he held that such humane legislation, in addition to reforming attitudes and enhancing social stability, would effect commercial expansion and generate power for the state.

Taken all in all, his projects reveal an awareness of structural weaknesses in state and society, and their coherence derives from the fact that they, directly or indirectly, promote a central political authority even as they attempt to reform public and private moral standards. In his appeal for linguistic reform, to give a more abstract example, besides describing the relation of speech to social responsibility and moral sensitivity, he understands the political effects of refined language. His suggestion that an academy should prove standards of acceptable and polite usage in terms of a simple rational model of communication acknowledges that, despite society's greater need for example than for pedantic legislation, the state still benefits from social recognition of linguistic reform. So, too, in proposing academies to persuade society about the nature of military prowess and virtues and to educate women to advance society's morals through the regulation of their families he implicitly makes it clear that the corollary of social and moral stability is the effectiveness of the state.

The final proposal in *An Essay upon Projects* concerning the regulation of the merchant and royal navies exemplifies well Defoe's opinion that the state must possess power sufficient to control labour and market conditions for the good of all and for the protection of the Revolution settlement. Upset that in war the monarch has to rely on incompetent pressed sailors and that in peace their scarcity permits merchant seamen to demand excessive wages, he urges a legislated reduction of wages and the introduction of a government registry of sailors which would guarantee them remuneration of an equal rate in the merchant and the royal service. In Defoe's mind the registry would guarantee the monarch competent war-time sailors and would ensure that unemployed seamen in peace would be retained and paid as if active sailors. By suggesting that government legislatively impose a cooperative trust on sailors Defoe can be seen to be simultaneously providing for philanthropy, commerce, and constitutional authority.

As well as underlying all his projects, his trust in the constitution's appropriateness to serve as an imperative to the restructuring of society informs the important social satire that he wrote during William's reign. For instance, the criticism of the upper classes in *The Poor Man's Plea* (1698) shows his realization that moral reformation depends upon officers of the state curbing their corruption and behaving with a sense that their good example is necessarily more effective than the mere imposition of the letter of the law upon the lower classes.

> *Laws are,* in Terrorem Punishments, *and Magistrates compel and put a Force upon Men's Minds; but Example is Persuasive and Gentle, and draws by a Secret, Invisible and almost Involuntary Power.* (Preface, /Al-v/)

His point here is that people with constitutional functions are obliged to initiate moral reform and to fulfill the potential for setting good examples which their social prominence gives to them. There were also particular historical reasons why the ruling classes had to reform themselves first. In his eyes, they had been contaminated by the immorality and Catholicism of the Stuart courts and, therefore, were bound to restore the 'Humanity' of Protestantism to public life. Through his spokesman he accuses the ruling classes of allowing attachment to their own interests to predominate over their commitment to the Protestant constitution. Specifically, he warns magistrates of the social consequences of their executing the law strictly upon the lower classes and with laxity upon their peers.

> 'Tis hard, Gentlemen, to be punish'd for a Crime, by a man as guilty as ourselves; and that the Figure a man makes in the World, must be the reason why he shall or shall not be liable to Law: This is really punishing men for being poor, which is no Crime at all; as a Thief may be said to be hang'd, not for the Fact, but for being taken. (p. 11)

He is sure that arbitrary administration of law discourages moral discrimination and prompts social anarchy in the minds of the poor. That the gentry could punish the poor for swearing, whoring, and drunkenness at the same time cultivating these vices as modish qualifications was intolerable to Defoe on account of the moral equivocation and the shallow assumptions about social structure entailed. Despite his satire of the actual gentry, however, he insists that the ruling classes should need no incitement to reform, that respect for the constitution should help truth to be irresistible to their consciences, and that their social superiority should make them morally superior to the poor whose social position reduces them to dependence on the example of their betters. To a certain extent, his insistence that the ruling classes must reform before their dependents and inferiors can be expected to is not in harmony with his having a poor man lecture his superiors about their need to reform. But this slight discrepancy is true to the nature of satire and heightens his sense that the ruling classes must reform as much for the benefit of the constitution as for the good of their souls.

Defoe also defended the constitution's significance to moral reformation by exposing another influential group of people in *The Villainy of Stock-Jobbers Detected* (1701). Instead of protecting public revenue and national credit, stock-brokers, according to him, were consumed with economic individualism: their speculation with Exchequer Bills brought about monetary instability, devaluation of paper credit, and specious stock prices. But it was not a matter of simple greed. He saw their speculation as partly a political strategy to embarrass William's administration. This political use of economic power to affect the constitution was completely unconstitutional in his estimation. Economic power was the tool of the state, but not of political parties: it could not be allowed to be a substitute for moral judgment and for the democratic ways of expressing political difference. Parliament had to suppress stock-jobbers, for their financial speculations were an attempt to diminish the state's control over imports, the movement of gold, and English manufacture. Their free-trade threatened to subvert general welfare as well as the parliamentary system. For Defoe, it was necessary to strengthen and refine the Revolution settlement because it was the constitution that had to dictate the terms on which trade and finance were honourable to the nation and consistent with the endeavour of moral reformation.

The ethical implications of the Revolution are nowhere more important than in his satirical treatment of dissent in *An Enquiry into the Occasional Conformity of Dissenters, In Cases of Preferment* (1698). As a Dissenter, Defoe frequently campaigned for religious toleration, but his sense of the constitution, among other things, made him careful about the terms of toleration. He did not think that the Dissenters should pretend to regulate themselves by the Law of Occasional Conformity, and what made him defend this position was an allegation that the dissenting Lord Mayor of London had coerced his non-dissenting attendant into carrying into a meeting-house the badge of office, which had been given to the Mayor on the condition of his being a conforming Anglican. In Defoe's eyes, the Mayor's intolerance and defiance of the terms of toleration were socially and constitutionally irresponsible: he had lost his credibility as a public officer and harmed the Dissenters' cause. This incident roused Defoe to argue that no true Dissenter can conform to the Anglican communion and that too many Dissenters, instead of benefiting from the Revolution's restriction of persecution, had become worldly and had forgotten that the constitution ensured their religious rights at the expense of some social rights. In Defoe's mind, the constitution gave Dissenters an extra reason to resist material privileges and to be resolute in the knowledge that

> Religion is the Sacred Profession of the Name of God; *serving him, believing in him, expecting from him*; and like the God it refers to, 'tis in one and the same object, one and the same thing perfectly indivisible and inseparable; there is in it no Neuter Gender, no Ambiguous Article, *God or Baal*; Mediums are impossible. (p. 11)

He maintains that, although the differences between modes of worship might seem to be merely circumstantial, their origin in conscience should ensure their preservation. A Dissenter, therefore, had to believe that his obedience to God was better fulfilled by serving in other than the Anglican church. Otherwise, he had no cause to be a Dissenter: 'Nay, he that cannot Dye, or at least desire to do so, rather than Conform, *ought to conform*' (p. 13). Defoe recommends that the Dissenters remember the Act of Toleration, which he considers as integral to the Revolution settlement, and forget the Bill for Occasional Conformity. By recognizing the moral force of the constitution the Dissenters could not but see that it was absurd to dissent and to conform and that in such inconsistency conforming implied the illegality of dissent and dissenting condemned the conscience that allowed conformity. From Defoe's viewpoint, those Dissenters who practised occasional conformity were obviously hypocritical and materialistic. Not only did they lack real faith and conscience but also they failed to see that respect for the political constitution of 1689 was an important means of strengthening and reforming their congregation. Their rationalization that occasional conformity should be considered simply as a civil action angered Defoe because it supposed a naive notion of morality and of the sacraments. He insisted that it was impossible to determine the morality of ordinary actions by their ends alone and contended that the same was true of religious actions: 'Some Actions are not Civil or Religious, as they are Civilly or Religiously perform'd, but as they are civil or religious in themselves' (p. 16). As a consequence, he held that the sacrament of communion had a wholly divine significance independently of whether it was celebrated in an Anglican or Dissenting service. This argument precludes an individual from regarding the sacrament as civil in one church and religious in the other. It also reinforces Defoe's position that Dissenters have no constitutional grounds to complain about the Law of Occasional Conformity. Defoe admitted that he himself did not like the law; he fully recognized that it represented religious discrimination in civil matters. But, if it had become part of the constitution, there was so much more in the constitution that fortified the Dissenters' civil and religious rights. In Defoe's judgment, the dissenting congregation was obliged to accept political restrictions as a religious duty to itself and as a social duty to provide others with an example of pure faith. In his way of thinking, the Dissenters would do more to promote understanding between the churches by maintaining a distinct constitutional and doctrinal identity than by choosing compromise. He judged that compromise, because it undermined moral, religious, and constitutional principles, eroded the only grounds on which true reformation could be founded.

Perhaps *The True-Born Englishman* is the most obvious example of his celebration of the Revolution settlement and of his urgent sense of moral reform. In this energetic poem, the most widely-read of the works which he composed in William's reign, he berates all sections of society with ingratitude to the King and offers a summary explication of his political reasons for regarding the Bill of Rights as the moral force capable of initiating a new social order. In hyperbolic style he satirizes the prejudices, affectations, and insular notions which he thought had brought about the irrational hostility towards William. He scorns the so-called purity of the English tradition, for example, by stressing the extent to which the racial origins of the English are various and mixed and by praising the achievements and virtues of foreigners. Besides suggesting that the Revolution settlement is cause enough for the English to admire the Dutch and all foreigners, he argues that to despise foreigners is tantamount to rejecting English accomplishments and to wishing for an economically and socially backward state. Willing as ever to introduce an economic perspective into his defence of the Revolution, he affirms that, whereas prejudice against the Dutch has to be merely a matter of self-interest, the national economic good and commercial growth can only be furthered by the new immigrants and the new international relations which the Revolution prompted.

One interesting feature of Defoe's rhetorical response to the Revolution in *The True-Born Englishman* is his willingness to let the one work contain both eulogy and satire. Indeed, his enthusiasm for the Revolution is testified to by the relative lack of modulation between his reductive and constructive stances. The intensity, for instance, with which he applies the motif of the origin of government is so high that, instead of plainly insisting that the English are as ignoble and sinful as other nations, which is all that the theme requires, it excoriates them in a way which suggests that Defoe is gratified by so reducing their self-respect. He uses scatological imagery to support his case that the fathers of the nation were only the dregs of invading armies which themselves were made up of the dregs of mankind:

> We have been Europe's Sink, the Jakes where she
> Voids all her Offal Out-cast Progeny.[23]

By overstating his contention that the original freeholders were obviously not deserving men, he does more than assault the ruling classes' pride in history, for he also gives implicit testimony to the emotional sense of a new beginning which the Revolution settlement can generate. By insisting that, from the scurvy warriors of William the Conqueror down to the whores and illegitimate lords of Charles II's court, the English ruling classes have been dominated by ignobility and immorality, Defoe is enabled to show that the English claim to be of noble descent is the joint effect of moral shortsightedness and political recalcitrance.

> A True-Born Englishman's a Contradiction,
> In Speech an Irony, in Fact a Fiction.
> A Banter made to be a Test of Fools,
> Which those that use it justly ridicules.
> A Metaphor intended to express
> A man *a-kin* to all the Universe.   (p. 53)

In tension, then, with his typical fusion of economic, political, and religious arguments on behalf of the Revolution is his attack on contemporary moral sense with its startling array of hyperbole, oxymoron, paradox, irony and other tropes.

The survey of English immorality in the second section of the poem is very sweeping. The poor are condemned as thriftless and mutinous while their betters, the clergy and gentry, are described as drunkards and blasphemers. Defoe confidently avows that the nation is obsessed with individualistic notions of liberty, property, and religion: it would seem that everyone is beyond the curative influence of the Revolution constitution. His retelling of the main events surrounding the Revolution is extremely anti-clerical. It certainly overemphasizes the influence of the non-jurors' political role. Furthermore, in affording the opportunity to express his political theory, it leads him to be very reductive about the source of regal authority.

> Titles are shadows, Crowns are empty things,
> The Good of Subjects is the End of Kings.   (p. 64)

The contempt he feels for kingship is not matched by a complementary respect for the English as subjects. Rather, corresponding to his vitriolic remarks about the political and moral evasiveness of the nation is a eulogy of King William which, on the one hand, idealises his simple humanity and, on the other, celebrates his transcendently religious character. So, while the second section of the poem allows Defoe to popularize his theoretical ideas about the original power of the people, the implicit contract between governor and governed, and the balance of power within the constitution, it also involves him in rhetorical contraries. Having declared that titles are empty things, he goes out of his way to create honorific names for William. Hence, the King is 'The Soul of War, and Life of Victory' and the one who 'Fights to Save, and Conquers to set Free' (p. 68). Clearly, the figurative energy of the eulogy of William is testimony to Defoe's sense of the Revolution's effect on himself. But his willingness to convey the gap between political theory and political practice constitutes an emotional expression about society's inadequacies. That, furthermore, Defoe can end the poem by following the celebration of William with the depiction of a sordid magistrate whose self-interest and irreligion could not be made more repulsive and whose inversion of the principles of the Revolution settlement could not be more thorough illustrates Defoe's rhetorical strategy for heightening his readers' emotional sense of the importance of the constitution.

Interestingly, the elegy which Defoe wrote for William, *The Mock-Mourners* (1702), contains a similar tension between satire and eulogy as a rhetorical means of emphasizing the principles and symbolic importance of the Revolution. Fierce again in his denunciation of national ingratitude, Defoe affirms with equal but opposite passion that William had singlehandedly restored the rights and liberties of England. He reveres the dead King as the archetypal hero, 'the very Mystery of War' (p. 91), whose integrity was providential and whose kindness was manifest in his constant desire to achieve reform. To Defoe, William had 'laid the first Foundation Stone' of the constitution (p. 83) and had been the only man able equally either 'To regulate the World, or conquer it' (p. 93).

The variety of rhetorical ways in which he sometimes stresses the curative effects and religious significance of the constitution itself and at other times emphasizes William's symbolic role and exemplary power provides convincing evidence of Defoe's commitment to the Revolution of 1688 and to moral reformation.

CHAPTER 4

Language and Narrative

'Tis true, Custom is allow'd to be our best Authority for Words, and 'tis fit it should be so; but Reason must be the Judge of Sense in Language, and Custom can never prevail over it. *Words*, indeed, like Ceremonies in Religion, may be submitted to the Magistrate; but *Sense*, like the Essentials, is positive, unalterable, and cannot be submitted to any Jurisdiction; 'tis a Law to it self, 'tis ever the same, even an Act of Parliament cannot alter it.

Words, and even Usages in Stile, may be alter'd by Custom, and Proprieties in Speech differ according to the several Dialects of the Countrey, and according to the different manner in which several Languages do severally express themselves.

But there is a direct Signification of Words, or a *Cadence in Expression*, which we call speaking *Sense*; this, like Truth, is sullen and the same, ever was and will be so, in what manner, and in what Language soever 'tis express'd.[1]

Although the occasion of this distinction between words and sense is Defoe's attempt to establish an argument by which he can discountenance fashionable cursing and swearing, his relation of linguistic to moral reform manifests itself widely in his writings. He was concerned frequently by the notion that people can 'speak in *Words*' and yet be 'perfectly unintelligible as to *Meaning*' and that they can talk without saying anything. This disjunction, however, between articulation and signification did not make him disgusted with the seeming arbitrariness of verbal meaning. For, as the epigraph shows, he appears comfortable in accepting it as an inevitable and natural fact that convention and change should dominate usage in a given speech community. What seems to have reconciled him to the relativity of words was a sense of linguistic universality: he was convinced that, if custom is the arbiter of usage, it is not the standard of meaning. Since sense was, in his view, absolute, permanent, and the same in all languages, it could only be assessed by reason. But, in addition to maintaining that, since sense is the proper object of reason, it is legitimate to be prescriptive about linguistic meaning, he provides a religious analogy to explain his distinction between words and sense. The analogy which is based on the difference between the worldly and divine aspects of religion contrasts the formal and substantive elements of language.

Hence, words are made equivalent to religious rites and sense to creed. His point is that words, like rites, are subject to human rules whereas sense exists beyond the scope of civil regulations. By this distinction, however, he is enabled to argue that words become the vehicles of sense as long as speakers respect the natural, rational, and unchanging rules which words must follow in their mutual interaction. Clearly, part of his campaign for moral reform was to insist that talking must become saying and that society must value the rules by which words are converted into sense. His own use of words and his themes about communication often exemplify this moral insistence and illustrate his continual desire to move beyond local and particular meaning to a more general significance.

A particularly revealing example of Defoe's using words to move beyond the particular to the general is his willingness to allude to John Wilmot, Earl of Rochester. He referred to the poet and his works over a long span of time: allusions occur as early as *The Poor Man's Plea* and as late as the unfinished *The Compleat English Gentleman*. To a limited extent, these allusions reveal his literary and social pretensions and his philosophical affinities.[2] But such explanations do not adequately account for the contrary functions that Rochester's name serves. Certainly, Defoe made few attempts to present a uniform and consistent image of the poet. Rather, he isolated facets of Rochester's character for general rhetorical purposes with the consequence that the poet could be called both 'that *Dog in a Doublet*' and 'that Man of Spirit.'[3] Indeed, Defoe used Rochester's name as an emblem of both the hardened atheist and the individual unable to stifle the promptings of his soul. So, on the occasion of arguing that spiritual health can be maintained only by a frequent and steady contemplation of death, Defoe heightens his tenets by objecting to Rochester's 'Atheistical' songs and by condemning the poet's avowed intention to deaden the minds of his readers to thoughts of death and judgment.[4] Yet, because Rochester was the type of the deliberately sinful person, Defoe could allude to him in order to emphasize the social aspects of immorality. Hence, in *The Poor Man's Plea* Defoe's spokesman comments that

> We find some People very fond of Monopolizing a Vice, they would have all of it to themselves; they must, as my Lord *Rochester* said of himself, *Sin like a Lord*; little sneaking Sins won't serve their turn; but they must be Lewd at a rate above the Common Size, to let the world see they are capable of it. (p. 18)

Here, besides giving it a wholly serious context, Defoe generalizes Rochester's confession: the poet is made to lend authority to Defoe's notion that sin is committed from perverse ideas of fashion and prestige. Moreover, Rochester's supposed death-bed conversion stood Defoe in good stead when he needed to cite an extreme example of divine favour to man.[5] Rochester's lewdness and unorthodox flouting of the Bible actually made it easier for Defoe to argue for the impossibility of atheism and the truth of grace. In addition to using references to Rochester to illustrate such doctrinal issues, Defoe applied the motif of the penitent poet in more controversial situations. For example, he seeks to discountenance a rival journalist by insisting that he ought 'to joyn my Lord *Rochester's* Confession to his Penitentials,—*I am a Rascal, that thou knowest!*'[6] and in a satire on hypocritical friendship, after quoting the same line, he suggests that the individual guilty of such a sin should apply the line to himself 'after my Lord *Rochester* in his Sarcasm upon a much honester Man.'[7] To Defoe, Rochester's confession that he had never been able to suppress his conscience, even as he committed his worst crimes, proved the poet to be honest. But he did not therefore revere the poet's name. Rochester remained a useful paradox in Defoe's rhetoric, a figure capable of lending emphasis to religious admonition and exhortation.

Defoe was as ambivalent about Rochester's writing as he was about the poet's character. But what Defoe's remarks about Rochester's poetry demonstrate is a desire to heighten rhetorical effects and to subordinate literary to moral judgment. For example, on one occasion he compares Rochester unfavourably with Milton by determining that the former's popularity stemmed from an irreligious exploitation of vulgar taste whereas the latter's sublime style derived from moral thinking. This comparison, because it is based on a wish to promote the reformation of manners, pays little attention to literary argument. In ascribing Rochester's wit to an addiction to wine and lewdness, Defoe is content to turn the poet into an emblem of evil and social decadence.[8] On another occasion, however, when he pretends to be competent to act as an apologist for the civilizing influence of poetry, he declares that Rochester is as capable as Milton of touching the soul.[9] Again, this comparison is remarkable less for its literary judgment than for its attempt to generate rhetorical authority. Even when he appears to be concerned just with Rochester's poems, he usually implies a moral perspective. For example, in the following passage where he denies Rochester's popularity, his description of the public's distaste for the poet is actually a prescription against the writers of Charles II's reign: Defoe's concession of moral sense to the public and of wit to the poet is a rhetorical strategy by which he can condemn Rochester in general, if implicit, terms.[10]

> Rochester's Poems, however castrated, and stript of the odious Nudities in which they at first appeared, have not been valued. The inimitable brightness of his Wit has not been able to preserve them from being thought

worthy, by wise Men, to be lost, rather than remember'd; being blacken'd and eclips'd by the Lewdness of their Stile, so as not to be made fit for Modesty to read or hear.[13]

With his own witty paradoxes Defoe belittles Rochester's wit, and his commitment to the moral justification of literature is obvious in the way in which he pretends to be so certain that the morally desirable reaction to Rochester is an accomplished fact. It is revealing to consider that, while in this passage Defoe denies Rochester's popularity for the avowed purpose of celebrating public taste, in the first comparison with Milton mentioned above he asserts the notorious poet's popularity in order to reprimand public taste! Far from saying anything about Rochester, the allusions to his poetry testify to the dialectical nature of Defoe's attitude towards his readers.

For the sake of appealing to his audience, Defoe would not praise Rochester's poetry without judging the poet. Indeed, it was to Defoe's rhetorical purposes to emphasize that Rochester was as exceptional a sinner as he was a poet. In a footnote to *Jure Divino*, he puts this paradox succinctly: 'In Wit and Crime the late Lord *Rochester* was hardly ever outdone by one Man in the World' (Bk. 1, p. 24). Moreover, Defoe obviously wanted to transform Rochester into a symbol of the opposite extremes of human potentiality. Hence, he goes on to stress the refinements of the poet's mind and his bodily bestiality.

> The Image of *Pan* too admirably suits the late Lord *Rochester*; Pan was Painted, half Man, half Goat; his upper Parts the Man, and his lower Part the Beast: Nothing can suit the Character better; he had a Head fill'd with the refined'st Wit, but the Vices of his other Part were Brutal and Intollerable justly suited to the Representation of a Goat, and abhor'd by all Good Men.

Defoe seizes upon Rochester's cultivated lack of integrity to create an emblem of unfulfilled human good. By mockingly converting Rochester into the god of poetry, Defoe makes him a satirical device for exposing the Restoration's moral and literary disorder and for rousing the reader to religious thoughts about death and eternity. From this example it is clear that Defoe used Rochester very much as he did Hobbes. From both notorious writers he borrowed analytical and reductive ideas for rhetorical purposes. But when he needed to bolster his satire of society he employed them as archetypes of irreligion.[12] His exploitation and generalization of their names shows that his eclecticism was aggressive and creative.

His moral impulse ensured that, when he actually cited Rochester's poetry, he did not do so merely for literary effect. As a consequence, he variously transforms Rochester's poetic effects.[13] In *Conjugal Lewdness*, for example, he refers to Rochester's poem 'The Fall' to help express his disgust with women who justify sexual licence in terms of necessity. That is, he censures married women who desire to remain childless and accuses them of loving their husbands for the 'frailer Part, as my Lord *Rochester* calls it' (p. 164). By totally ignoring the context of the poem and by extracting Rochester's phrase as if it had been intended to be a decent euphemism rather than a sexual innuendo, Defoe appears to respect the poet for being a linguist and moral authority.[14] When he repeats this allusion to 'The Fall', he even praises Rochester for 'modestly' expressing his sentiment (p. 231). It is interesting, therefore, that, earlier in *Conjugal Lewdness*, Defoe harshly refuses to repeat a scandalous poem that had been attributed to Rochester (p. 96); instead, he insists that Rochester's poetry corrupts sexual morality. From these examples of his citation of Rochester it should be clear that Defoe would not consider the poetry in and for itself and that he used it for rhetorical emphasis by diminishing or heightening the poet's sentiments. An intention of presenting the reader with a constant impression of the poet could not have been further from Defoe's mind. Rather, the poet served as a figure to clarify or exemplify moral problems, and it was in order to sustain a moral focus that Defoe either removed Rochester's poetic statements from their bawdy contexts or emphasized and exacerbated the poet's gross intentions.

Certainly, there are many times when, because he wished to deflate the notion of human dignity as a means of introducing moral exhortation into his writing, Defoe cites lines from Rochester which are reductive about human nature without passing comment on the poet. In *Serious Reflections*, for example, Robinson Crusoe quotes twelves lines from 'A Satyr against Reason and Mankind' to convince a devout gentlewoman about the degeneracy of mankind (p. 112). Again, when he embraces the poet's view that 'Fear is the original Cause of Courage' to support his contentions that common soldiers face death not from principle but from sheer social coercion and that human behaviour cannot be dignified on its own terms, Defoe feels no need to comment on either the poet or the context of his remark.[15] But usually, because his citations of Rochester attempt to do more than exploit notions of fallibility, they tend to imply criticism of the poet by serving moral proposals. For example, as part of a campaign on behalf of the priority of religious conscience for which he maintains that confession of sin is less frightening than going into battle, he remarks that since 'all Shame is Cowardise, as an eminent Poet tells us, That all Courage is Fear, the bravest Spirit is the best qualify'd for a Penitent' (*Serious Reflections*, p. 28). But Rochester's dictate is not analogous or parallel to Defoe's. For, whereas the poet reduces a virtue to a weakness, Defoe equates timidity of conscience to physical fear in order to devise the positive prescription that really heroic people inevitably practise confession. Defoe might agree with Rochester that men are physical cowards, but his insistence that all men are potential moral heroes is definitely not the poet's view. Since the result of his oblique reference to Rochester is the affirmation that spiritual resolution cannot be regarded from the perspective of physical courage, it is possible to judge that Defoe's seeming analogy effects a transformation of the poet's dictate.

Although he seems to depend on the epigrammatic force of Rochester's lines, Defoe makes the rhetorical situations which they serve so dominant that the consequent extension of the meaning of the lines often leads to moral admonitions that are totally unrelated to Rochester's poetry. Consider the following lines from 'Artemisia to Chloe':

> A Woman's ne'er so ruin'd, but she can
> Revenge herself on her Undoer Man.[16]

On one occasion, these lines are cited to reinforce a warning to weavers that, if they continue to abuse women for buying imported clothes, the women will ruin the weavers by making their own clothes.[17] On another occasion, Defoe quotes the lines to reconcile the nation to setbacks in the war with France and to assure his audience that, as long as King William's foreign policies are implemented, eventual victory is guaranteed.[18] Defoe also repeats these lines in an episode in *The Great Law of Subordination* (1724) the purpose of which is to discourage whoring and drunkenness. In this episode, a woman who has been seduced while drunk retaliates by getting her seducer drunk and then marrying him. The latter announces on waking that his new wife has made '*Lord* Rochester's *Verses good upon*' him (p. 69). On these three occasions Defoe pays little attention to the poetic context of the cited lines or to Rochester's sentiments. Instead, his own rhetorical intentions endow the lines with an imperative, reforming value. Even Moll Flanders alludes to and cites the lines from 'Artemisia to Chloe' to justify the strategy by which she secures her acquaintance's right to inspect the character of her suitor (pp. 68 and 72). But by citing these lines she also is enabled to make her appeal to women to look after their own interests. Rochester's lines serve Moll as a slogan in her exhortation to reformation. To an extent Moll is like her creator because she exploits Rochester's poetry to further moral ideas which are at odds with the poetry. That she, like Defoe, is capable of criticizing the poet implicitly is obvious when she makes another allusion to him as a way of explaining her instinctive recoil from the degraded people of The Mint. Discontent with possessing the reputation of a whore from residing in The Mint and unhappy that she does not enjoy the material benefits that whores usually receive, she contemplates Rochester's 'Song to Phyllis' as a means of spurring herself to leave The Mint. She parallels herself to the poet's mistress whom she judges to have rejected the poet's terms for a liaison (p. 64). Despite her ignorance of traditional morality, then, her latent good sense is demonstrated by the way in which she transforms Rochester's poem into an imperative at the same time implying criticism of the poet's immorality.

The latitude with which Defoe refers to Rochester is more than a matter of changing or disregarding the poet's character and of altering the arguments and contexts of his poems. It is perhaps, more fundamentally, a matter of his turning the poet's 'Words a little awry.'[19] For, while by choosing Rochester's words Defoe is enabled to generate the rhetorical stance of a worldly and literary man, by adapting them at the same time he can achieve a moral stance which implies the limitations of Rochester's views and which is more significant than a rhetorical appeal. Consider the striking example when Defoe adopts the whimsical and reductive third and fourth lines of 'A Satyr against Reason and Mankind' to lend support by analogy to a serious argument about spiritual agency. He maintains that spirits may be like 'what my Lord *Rochester* expresses in another Case,

> *A spirit free to chuse for their own Share*
> *What Case of Flesh and Blood they please to wear.*'[20]

In this case, an irreverently facetious hypothesis is used to illustrate a straightforward explanation of the nature of angels. Obviously, Defoe enjoys adapting Rochester's words to his own purposes. Mentioning Rochester's name and title with respect and admitting the difference between his own and the poet's verbal usage, Defoe can still, because of his moral confidence, apply the lines to his own rhetorical uses.

Most frequently his references to Rochester are employed by Defoe to project the image of a confident, accomplished writer. He often cites those of the poet's lines which he can adapt to illustrate the hazards of authorship and with which he can make a direct appeal to the sympathy of his audience by testifying that his own steadfastness and integrity have helped him to overcome or to ignore such hazards. In *Conjugal Lewdness*, for example, he cites the following lines,

> *Nor shall weak Truth your Reputation save,*
> *The Knaves will all agree to call you Knave.* (p. 17),

to heighten his justification of writers whose necessary exposure of vice makes them vulnerable to the insults of the vicious members of the audience. Besides using these lines to reinforce the image of himself as a resolute, conscientious moralist, thereby implicitly criticizing Rochester's notion of *'weak Truth'*, he also defended his own integrity as a political commentator by pretending to be able to convert his opponents' criticism into praise: 'I am so far from being Concern'd at their Reproaches, that, as my Lord *Rochester* said in another Case, *I count their Censure FAME.*'[21] On other occasions, he employed this citation to help declare his religious integrity as a writer and to profess a sense of superiority over the detractors of his economic journalism.[22] Setting aside his moral contempt for the poet for a moment, it is possible to claim that Defoe recognized in the epigrammatic and hyperbolic expression of Rochester's poetry a boldness and resilience of diction which he wanted to translate into his own rhetorical strategies. By referring to Rochester, Defoe heightened the sensitivity and the resoluteness of his narrative stance:

> Such be my Lot while I live, *viz*. To speak home and Impartially, to tell both Sides their Mistake, though at the Purchase of their mutual Curses; my Lord *Rochester* tells this is the sure Fate of a Plain Dealer.[23]

By seeming to accept the isolated position of the moral writer Defoe tries to establish sympathy for himself and by treating Rochester as if he is a literary authority Defoe attempts to win the respect that comes from being comprehended by literary tradition. That, however, Defoe in various ways converted Rochester into a rhetorical figure cannot disguise the fact that he felt superior to the poet. An episode in *The Political History of the Devil* nicely reveals this fact. In this episode a lord and servant debate Rochester's attitude towards oaths (pp. 300-02). The servant wins the debate by citing some anonymous lines against his master's professed atheism: the lines, concerning the common sense of believing in the after-life, are Defoe's.[24] This covert subjection of Rochester to himself shows that, as regards doctrine and creed, Defoe had little respect for Rochester: it also exemplifies Defoe's habit of quoting himself in a restrained and undemonstrative way. However, by presenting Rochester as support for his rhetorical stance Defoe shows not just the unsystematic and flexible method by which he reinforced his persuasiveness but also a continual desire to extend Rochester's particular words into general and moral meaning.

Although, on account of moral and doctrinal reasons, Defoe preferred Milton to Rochester, he was far from being consistently respectful in his allusions to Milton. In particular, Defoe was critical of *Paradise Lost*. Yet in finding fault with Milton's very endeavour to retell the biblical story in the epic tradition, Defoe reveals a shrewd understanding of the relation between the formal demands of narrative and their effect on religious truth. To begin with, Defoe found the implied narrative viewpoint in the poem inherently absurd and presumptuous. The circumstantiality of the narrative in such scenes as Satan's temptation of Eve upset Defoe because it made it so obvious that the implicit claim to omniscience could not be granted.[25] In Defoe's eyes, Milton's attempt to represent and to detail transcendent religious matters exceeded the function of narrative. As he makes plain, however, in *The Political History of the Devil*, he did not take exception to the way in which Milton makes Satan seduce Eve by whispering in her ear while she is asleep, for this depiction conformed to verifiable psychological truth (p. 443). But the relevance and immediacy of this depiction just served to heighten his awareness that other properties which Milton employed in the seduction scene were beyond conception. Basing his reaction upon St. Paul's tacit response to his experience of the third heaven, Defoe is moved to argue that Milton's narrative is testimony that the poet could not have recognized the true nature of the ineffable (p. 441). Since he held that neither reason nor the understanding can deal with inexpressible religious phenomena, Defoe judged it irresponsible of Milton to compose his epic as if such phenomena were within the reach of the senses and of narrative embodiment.

In addition to discovering an unacceptable positivism in the poet's narrative expression, on several occasions in *The Political History of the Devil* Defoe suggests that Milton's commitment to narrative was unthinking to the extent that it involved him in unorthodox theological positions and actually caused him to confuse Christian doctrines. He chooses, for example, to comment on Milton's 'fiction' of Satan's 'refusing to acknowledge and submit to the Messiah' (p. 295). Indeed, he condemns it as 'strain'd' and 'fine-spun.' From Defoe's viewpoint, Milton's desire to be realistic by giving motives to Satan had blurred his view of doctrinal issues and showed the poet's lack of moral authority. Confident in his orthodox stance, Defoe insists that Satan could not have been envious of Christ's power in Heaven before the creation of man, as Milton has it, since Christ was not given universal power until after the resurrection. Defoe is adamant that Satan's rebellion is attributable to causes other than the envy of Christ which Milton proposes, yet at the same time he maintains that such causes are unknowable. On another occasion, Defoe finds Milton 'grossly erroneous' for having God the Father beget the Son before the fall of Satan and the creation of man. Drawing on established biblical commentators, Defoe urges that the begetting of the Son could have happened only at the incarnation or resurrection (p. 310). His sense that the poet's narrative could do nothing to clarify such doctrinal problems as the origin of evil in Heaven caused him to be wholly ironical in his descriptions of the aesthetic appeal of Milton's 'fine Images and lofty Excursions' and of his 'most formal, solemn manner.' Convinced that the translation of the biblical narrative into the idiom of the epic was impossibly pretentious and showed up the merely artificial nature of the poet's formality and solemnity, Defoe was also sure that it represented, more seriously, an ignoring of the traditional knowledge of the prophets and an assertiveness which defied divine knowledge (p. 336). Indeed, because he could not concur with the traditional literary notions that poetic licence is unbounded and that a poet cannot be accused of blasphemy, he frequently indicates the essential redundancy and presumption of Milton's poem. Often he sarcastically states that Milton tells God what God already and alone knows. On one such occasion he suggests that Milton compliments

> God *Almighty* with a flux of lofty words, and great sounds, and has made a very fine Story of the *Devil*, but he has made a mere *je ne scay Quoi* of *Jesus Christ*.

By being facetious and playfully affected in his exposure of the hollowness of Milton's style, Defoe is enabled to express his disgust about the fact that the poet has expended more effort in depicting Satan than in presenting Christ. He criticizes Milton, then, for demeaning Christ by giving in to the demands of plot and narrative: he finds it ridiculous that, as a consequence of presenting an interesting image of Satan, Milton should be willing to depict Christ addressing his saints at a time when there could have been none. Defoe is also critical of Milton's amplified treatment of setting in Heaven and Hell because, aside from suggesting misdirected energy, its concentration on physical and graphic elements seems to be absurdly realistic and an evasion of historical truth. Clearly, Defoe is unhappy that Milton should have subordinated the Bible to principles of literary selectiveness. He also felt that, by creating the precedent of underemphasizing certain portions of the Bible, Milton might encourage people to ignore all of the Bible (p. 339). Defoe certainly recognized that it was, for instance, a requirement of graphic narrative to depict a physical setting for Hell. But he judged that, because Milton's narrative pretends that Hell is a locatable prison from which Satan can escape physically, the poet's concern for aesthetic pleasure actually displaced the idea that Hell is primarily a mental state and worked against the biblical notion, evident in the story of Job, that Satan is a powerful enemy because he is a prisoner at large (p. 344). For Defoe, Milton's setting debased the ideas of Hell and Satan, as well as the figure of Christ.

While Defoe criticizes the licence with which Milton applies narrative to the Bible, he does not restrict himself to a literal-minded view of the Scriptures. Indeed, he often examines the meaning of the Bible from a narrative perspective: the deductions he draws from words and the inferences he educes from setting about antecedents and consequences show that he cultivated narrative for exegetical and homiletic purposes. In *The Political History of the Devil*, for instance, although he concedes that there is 'no Authority in Scripture' to assert that the murder of Abel involved the killing of Abel's family, he insists upon its likelihood (p. 374). He supposes that Cain and Abel had fathered children and proposes that, since Abel's posterity is nowhere mentioned, the family of Cain had killed Abel's survivors to remove the possibility of revenge. Clearly, Defoe recognizes that probability belongs to interpretation: he is certainly comfortable dealing with positive and negative textual evidence as a means of expatiating about setting and motive. Moreover, for rhetorical purposes he often approaches biblical stories with a keen sense of relevance: he makes it plain that the worldly setting of these stories is equivalent to contemporary society and he spends considerable energy in persuading his readers to accept his amplifications of biblical settings. Hence, in the abovementioned work, he appeals to his readers to realize how Noah must have been abused when he began to build the ark by cogitating about the way in which religious zeal is insulted in contemporary life. By passing on to detail how Noah must have been reviled Defoe extends the biblical narrative with the obvious intention of making it serve satirical and homiletic goals (pp. 378-79).

If his practice of expatiation illustrates that Defoe regarded biblical verses as condensed narratives, he is never overly determinate about setting or motive. As in his version of the story of Abel, his expatiation is usually based upon a desire to generalize. So, also, when he expands upon the feelings and experiences which Noah enjoyed after the Flood and when he elaborates upon the incident of Noah's drunkenness, he emphasizes the typicality of what happens. Thus, he explains that Canaan, the son of Ham, was a fit agent to seduce Noah into drunkenness because, since his father was not as religious as Noah's other sons, Japhet and Shem, he must have had a superficial education (p. 383). Furthermore, his speculations about the physical setting in which Noah lived are far from whimsical. Rather they heighten the moral significance of Noah's fall from divine favour because in their very plainness they diminish the merely shocking aspects of the story. Hence, he insists that Noah must have known about viniculture before the Flood and that a good many years must have elapsed after the Flood for Canaan to grow to manhood and to be able to seduce Noah. Defoe also infers that as the moral leader of the day Noah must have had much experience in preaching against the evil effects of wine. By expatiating on such matters Defoe emphasizes Noah's responsibility for his own disgrace in order to argue against those biblical commentators and readers who, feeling sympathy for Noah, would reduce his guilt. His narrative stress upon Noah's loss of moral integrity and upon his betrayal of the role of the preacher is a justification of the orthodox notion that there was a break in the tradition of spiritual leaders which obliged God to speak directly to Abraham (p. 386). By claiming to follow up narrative clues and to make narrative connections Defoe sets out to vindicate the biblical account against those who would misread or sensationalize it. His similar treatment of the story of Noah in *A System of Magick* reinforces this conclusion. Here he decries Noah as the 'drunken Monitor' who undermined the effects of his teaching by causing people to compose ballads about him rather than to follow his good example (pp. 14-15). Defoe again stresses that, while by the single incident of drunkenness Noah surrendered his moral leadership, he was not surprised into sin. In a way that typically exploits narrative contraries Defoe heightens the finality of the consequences of Noah's drunkenness together with the ordinariness of the circumstances in which the incident unfolded (p. 97). By giving the reader scope to wonder in plain terms about geographical setting and about the likely ambivalence of Canaan's motives for seducing Noah, Defoe is enabled to employ his narrative expatiation to serve his moral perspective.

Critical to Defoe's sense of the limits of permissible expatiation upon biblical texts is his awareness of words. His narrative deductions often display both a diachronic and a synchronic understanding of verbal meaning: that is, his biblical interpretation is usually based upon the assumptions that words have a history that parallels the temporal development of society and that within a speech community the meaning of a word depends upon the range of its usages. In *A System of Magick*, for example, Defoe surveys the various biblical uses of the word 'seer' and is able to demonstrate the specialization and the melioration of the word as it moves in historical stages from referring to a merely learned man to designating ultimately a man of God. In addition, his references in this work to biblical commentators show his understanding of the importance of semantics to exegesis: he is clearly aware that he must expatiate upon 'emphatic significant Expression' if he is to reveal spiritual meaning. Hence, he realizes that the expression 'walk with God' signifies, because of its context and usage, faithful behaviour rather than something more concrete (p. 12). Furthermore, his awareness of the semantic flexibility of words, namely, that one word may possess more than one referent and one grammatical function at the same time, contributes considerably to his explication of doctrinal matters. He appreciates that semantic variability frees him from rigid theoretical positions and allows him to exploit narrative contraries to the best advantage. In *The Political History of the Devil*, for example, he announces his satisfaction that the word 'devil' is both a proper noun and a common name, that it refers to one and to many spirits, and he traces the singular and plural signification of the noun to Christ's confrontation with Legion.[26] But, in addition to this diachronic sense of the word 'devil,' Defoe also takes advantage of the contemporary usage of the word according to which it is extended to refer to anything evil:

> Thus we take the name of *Devil* to signify not persons only, but actions and habits; making imaginary Devils, and transferring that substantial creature called DEVIL, into every thing noxious and offensive. (p. 315)

Through being able to use one word variously Defoe can demythologize the devil while stressing the reality of the principle of evil, and as he indicates the negative and disintegrating effects of evil he can illustrate the interconnectedness of evil phenomena.

A concern for how words work is also a prominent feature of Defoe's development of secular narrative. An examination of the attention he pays to language reveals his sense of how this sort of narrative should establish meaning. For instance, he continually draws the reader to notice names, their designation, and their status. He emphasizes at the same time the various factors which affect naming and calling. Yet, his frequent exposition of the historical, geographical, social, and cultural influences upon words is not only a major trait of his narrative style, for it is also related to his important thematic attempts to connect talking and saying. Consider the following paragraph from *A Tour through the Whole Island of Great Britain*.

> In this Inlet of the Sea is *Osey* or *Osyth* Island, commonly called *Oosy* Island, so well known by our *London* Men of Pleasure, for the infinite Number of Wild-Fowl, that is to say, Duck, Mallard, Teal and Widgeon, of which there are such vast flights, that they tell us the Island, Namely the Creek, seems covered with them, at certain times of the Year, and they go from *London* on purpose for the Pleasure of Shooting, and indeed often come Home very well loaden with Game. But it must be remembred too, that those Gentlemen who are such lovers of the Sport, and go so far for it, often return with an *Essex* Ague on their Backs, which they find a heavier Load than the Fowls they have shot. (I, p. 11)

Here is an example of Defoe's typical way of recording proper names. He frequently shows that one place has more than one proper name. Moreover, it is also typical that he should distinguish between proper and common names. Not only does this attention to names contrast traditional and contemporary ways of designating, for also, more generally, it illustrates the arbitrariness of names and implies that there is no one-to-one relation between names and things. Obviously, it was not Defoe's habit to employ single names in order to make his narrative seem realistic. Much more representative of his narrative goals, on the other hand, is the elaboration of the different species of birds after the announcement of the class name and before the use of a different class name as a common plural. This implicit stress on the flexibility of naming is reinforced by the emphasis Defoe gives to the fact that the hunters use the word for the whole to refer to a part of the island. This instance exemplifies Defoe's expository habit of insisting that point of view determines the manner in which words are used. Finally in this paragraph, the attention given to the variable function and usage of words gives a heightened effect to the verbal wit by which Defoe transfers 'Load' into a metaphor of 'Ague.' This verbal dexterity serves to hint his judgment about the rewards of pleasure.

Defoe was very aware of the importance to narrative of sense transference and its causes, as the following passage will help to prove.

> On this Shoar also are taken the best and nicest, tho' not the largest Oysters in *England;* the Spot from whence they have their common Appellation is a little Bank called *Woelfleet,* scarce to be called an Island, in the mouth of the River *Crouch,* now called *Crooksea Water;* but the chief Place where the said Oysters are now had, is from *Wyvenhoo* and the Shoars adjacent whither they are brought by the Fishermen, who take them at the Mouth of, that they call, *Colchester* Water, and about the Sand they call the *Spits,* and carry them up to *Wyvenhoo,* where they are laid in Beds or Pits on the Shoar to Feed, as they call it; and then being barrelled up, and carried to *Colchester,* which is but three Miles off, they are sent to *London* by Land, and are, from thence, called *Colchester* Oysters. (I, p. 12)

The main point of the paragraph is that Colchester oysters have derived their name not from being caught, bred, or boxed at Colchester but from the London market's having them transported from Colchester. Yet there is other evidence in the paragraph that reveals Defoe's concern to explain the imprecision of names. He shows, for example, that historical as well as geographical factors remotivate names. As a consequence, inevitable to his sense of narrative is exposition of how material forces are inseparable from verbal designation. Furthermore, his references to the activity of calling emphasize that, despite the variability of proper and common nouns, people are dependent upon words for their relation to reality. Defoe clearly implies that, although words are not absolute in reference or function, they are inevitably necessary to the control of material circumstance. Recognition of the functional necessity of sense transference and of the specialization of general terms does not lead him to be unrigorous about denotation. Hence, while an oyster may be said to feed, a sand-bank cannot be called an island. This paragraph, however, through its eight references to designation, most importantly manifests that Defoe's sense of narrative is inseparable from his appreciation of polysemy and semantic principles.

Throughout the first volume of *A Tour through the Whole Island of Great Britain* there are many representative instances of Defoe's narrative reliance upon the exposition of names, designations, and transferred meanings. For example, he frequently focusses his attention upon dialect and often advises the reader that trades and professions employ distinctive words and give specialist senses to common terms. Hence, he affirms that what city people call faggots woodsmen name ostrey wood (p. 101), that Norfolk graziers call Scottish cattle runts (p. 65), and that ship-builders refer to the working of wood as converting it (p. 108). By continually establishing such connections between standard speech and dialect, Defoe is enabled to project an informed narrative stance and one that is overtly concerned to promote mutual understanding. Yet he certainly appreciates the verbal inventiveness of dialect and recognizes that it can contribute to received expression. For instance, he is intrigued that seamen can apply the verb 'to reign' to the lasting stoutness of a vessel (p. 40) and that, by turning a noun into a verb, they can talk of a ship's ability to weather sea and storm (p. 70). His concession that, when he describes the coastal regions, he will employ the place names familiar to the local people and that, when he reports on the hinterland, he will use the proper names that are accepted there constitutes a tolerance of regional dialects and evidences his willingness to accommodate his narrative stance to linguistic phenomena. That, however, he often provides alternative names, equivalent expressions, and contextual definitions shows that by using and going beyond dialect at the same time he intended to appeal to both particular and general audiences.

His perpetual references to verbal usage reveal that by discoursing about words he aimed to use his narrative to educate his readers about the point of view that is inherent in diction. He often stresses that words are not neutral. So, for example, he emphasizes that, while the fashionable people of Tunbridge retire, he himself simply comes away (p. 128) and that, whereas the needy towns of the south coast practice commerce, in the eyes of the state they are guilty of smuggling or roguing (p. 206). Interestingly, he does criticize dialect if it confuses the point of view which is implicit in expressions. Hence, in reporting that the people of Swole (or Southole) cure sprats, he condemns their calling the process 'making red sprats' and suggests that they should say 'making sprats red' (p. 55). Aware of the gap between the processors' usage and meaning and that in their sense 'red' cannot be an attributive adjective, his objection is to the presumption of the popular expression.

His reaction to the blurring of nominal and real categories is prescriptive because he believed in the possibility of words saying new things. He held, for instance, that it is permissible to call the wheatear the English ortolan on the grounds that the native bird is as delicious as the foreign one (p. 127). By suggesting this new name he proposes that the wheatear should be thought of as a new thing. Yet, he clearly understood the dangers of this verbal licence: he knew that neither words nor particular usages of words need refer to or establish anything substantive. He thought of the noun 'fireball' as redundant and unscientific, preferring to speak the language of nature by talking of lightning striking a steeple (p. 134). In this disqualification of a popular noun, he states that the referent is a process rather than a determinable phenomenon and so requires a phrase rather than a substantive. Frequently, his discussion of what is permitted to be said shows a clear distinction between words and things. Indeed, he will not countenance nouns and transferred meanings unless there are strong grounds of experiential and scientific verification. Hence, he is scornful of people who can call petrified wood iron because they fail to see that they could provide no evidence to justify their verbal usage (p. 30). The occasions, however, when Defoe is critical of the extension of meaning and of the creation of words simply illustrate by contrast the times when he acclaims such verbal licence. He himself certainly tries to use words in a way that works against the tendency which particular communities have of insulating themselves by developing self-centred expression (p. 118). He opposes to such exclusive uses of language the realization that structural and technological changes within the larger community invalidate certain local words and attitudes. For example, he stresses that military engineering has displaced the traditional rhetoric of fortifications (p. 230). Of course, Defoe's penchant for testing new denotations against scientific standards does not rule out the use of metaphors: houses may still be called nests (p. 36) and a character may be said to be shipwrecked (p. 127). For he did not draw attention to naming and calling to impose a positivistic criterion on verbal usage. Rather he did so in order to convey the moral responsibility that is involved with the use of language. He understood, for instance, that talking about things entails both creating and changing them. So, he acknowledged that to say that a given town is in a state of decay is not to be regarded as a mere verbal concession since the concession is testimony to a changed state of affairs and is, therefore, implicated with things. With his frequent concessive qualification of propositions and descriptions, in such phrases as 'one might say' and 'it may be said,' Defoe is not being literal-minded about things. Rather he is implying that naming becomes saying by conventional agreement and that, through social cohesiveness, language performs as well as conveys meaning. One of the chief marks of his narrative style is to call attention to the possibilities of naming and saying as a means of soliciting agreement and of suggesting that his tentative designations might deserve to be made public ones. In *A Tour through the Whole Island of Great Britain*, as in other narratives, his concern with naming is partly attributable to his reforming zeal. He celebrates and amends the way in which the world is categorized and by stressing the variability of verbal categories he encourages new perceptions and conceptions.

His major fictional characters share several of Defoe's linguistic mannerisms and habits, but that their verbal usage is shown to be deficient as well as authoritative constitutes important evidence of how, by employing language to heighten narrative contraries, he can emphasize his social themes. Like her creator, Moll Flanders continually calls attention to names and to the way in which things are called what they are. By reporting that the people she can first remember are '*Gypsies* or *Egyptians*' she manifests an appreciation of the variability of names (p. 9); by announcing the two names of a major street she proves her awareness of received and vulgar usage (p. 160); and, by defining a 'Wherry' as a cross-channel ferry and as a small Thames row-boat she reveals that, besides understanding that a single thing may have more than one name, she realizes that one name may apply to more than one thing (p. 265). What authority Moll has as a commentator also derives partly from her knowledge of dialect and idiom. For instance, she often elaborates upon legal language. Through her treatment of context she conveys the sense of 'arraign'd' (p. 284), 'Dead Warrant' (p. 289), and 'Recognizances' (p. 277), while she fully defines 'Seize' as the creditor's legal right to secure debtors' goods by way of compensation for losses (p. 63). The authority of Moll's definitions is exemplified by the consideration that her explanation of a 'Gentleman-Tradesman' as a 'Land-water-thing' is exactly the one Defoe himself gives.[27] But, offsetting her precision with names and words is Moll's vagueness. For example, she cannot be sure whether the people who ordered her into service were called magistrates (p. 10) or whether what effected the banker's divorce was called a decree (p. 270). That she does not discover the meaning of 'Geographical' until she writes her account (p. 327) is another sign that Defoe intended to make Moll as unreliable as she is reliable. Furthermore, her explanations of idioms often illustrate her remoteness from conventional and current usage. When she refers to being 'put to Nurse, as they call it' (p. 9) and to 'going to Service, as they call'd it, that is to be a Servant' (p. 10) she demonstrates an inability, both as character and narrator, to share in social expressions. Of course, when she claims that 'I was mightily made of, as we say' (p. 17) and when she adopts the idioms 'a wet Day' (p. 118) and 'to the last Gasp' (p. 191) to heighten the pathetic image she projects, Defoe is content to stress her appealing ordinariness. But, most often, it is to his purpose to emphasize the remoteness with which she explains idioms.

Moll's use of words is both creative and irresponsible. By making her inconsistent in her verbal usage Defoe intends to induce the reader to respond to the themes she illustrates rather than to her character. Thus, when she uses 'Bargains' for thefts (p. 215) and 'going Abroad' instead of stealing (p. 253), the reader recognizes in Moll the desire to invert conventional and social meaning and to avoid moral responsibility. Even as a young girl, although, along with her peers, she calls her first protector nurse (p. 10), she creates her own names for the nurse in a manner that is equally assertive and defensive. Ironically, while she is ignorantly upset when she is entitled 'Miss,' she refers to her protector as 'my Mistress Nurse' (p. 12). At the same time her sense of what a gentlewoman is is also exposed (p. 14). Even as narrator her verbal usage lapses. Hence, when she alludes to *'that Cheat call'd LOVE'* (p. 60), her inversion of substantive and complement reveals an illogical, as well as shallow, cynicism. Frequently, however, both as character and narrator, Moll develops categorical reasons for extending or changing names: she recognizes that she ought to call her nurse mother (p. 16), that the man who refuses to have his character examined should be named a 'Rogue' (p. 70), and that living common law constitutes a 'felonious Treaty' (p. 107). While her creative use of words justifies her role as social satirist, her irresponsible usage betokens the causes of her typical immorality.

Moll's statements about language considered together with her verbal usage exemplify Defoe's concern with why speaking should always lead to significant saying. Since Moll is alert to the possibility that people can speak 'of meer Course, without any Meaning' (p. 27), Defoe implies that, to a certain degree, she understands that there are performative, intentional aspects to meaning. But, if she is critical of verbal insincerity, she is not proof against it. Consequently, she is overwhelmed by the fine words of her seducer, even though she recognizes their 'Circumlocution' (pp. 25-26). Moreover, when she pretends to Robert's mother that her second son's address to herself constitutes simply 'a wild airy way of Discourse that had no Signification in it' (p. 45), Moll applies her general awareness of the difference between speaking and saying evasively and immorally: not only is she wrong, but she exploits discourse which has no meaning in order to prevaricate. Although, as in the case where she emphasizes her argument that women must not take men's marriage proposals at face value, she demonstrates considerable powers of logic and reasoning (p. 75), she is also susceptible to rhetoric. Moved by the arguments of the older brother as to why she should marry Robert, she can neither resist nor repeat them (p. 55). Similarly, she finds the eloquence of her governess bewitching (p. 172). Her habit of praising the rhetoric of other people illustrates her tendency to avoid creating moral expression for herself. When, for instance, she claims that the banker's words are irresistible, her conversation with him reveals a good deal of playful, if conventional, verbal resistance together with a clear indication that she intends and wills his words to be irresistible (p. 180). This gap between commentary on language and exploitation of words is the cause of her hypocrisy and of much of her unhappiness. She realizes, as in the case with her brother, that words can be obliging and can establish personal bonds, but she prefers, on account of self-interest, to ignore this realization and to adopt the simple-minded maxim that people who are talkers are not doers and that those who are doers are not talkers in dealing with him (pp. 90 and 103). That her brother does talk and act desperately, shows up her need to consider the relation between speaking and saying more carefully. Defoe, however, makes her learn about the significance of speech negatively. Hence, after the revelation of the mutual deception between Jemmy and herself, she is shocked into a speechlessness which involves an unawareness of her own identity (p. 148). But her experience in Newgate suggests that she develops a more positive sense of the integrity of language. After she appreciates that her prayers are ineffective because they consist of 'Ordinary Expression' (p. 283), she learns to develop 'a kind of view into the other Side of time' which allows the 'Word Eternity' to represent 'itself with all its incomprehensible Additions' (p. 287). But, if her prayers are sincere for a short while because she uses language to perform meaning and to match moral intention, her verbal usage never becomes consistently moral. Indeed, by using Moll's inconsistent speech to illumine her ambiguous moral condition, Defoe is better able to exploit the narrative for his various social themes.

Like Moll, Robinson Crusoe frequently refers to names and naming. Yet, at the same time as his sense of language gives him credibility it is also responsible for a thematic dialectic which is more authoritative than his character. On the one hand, then, Crusoe remarks knowingly about usage and the anglicization of his own name (p. 3), records an interest in the relation of proper names when, for example, he reports that sailors call Africa Guinea (p. 16), and occasionally defines dialect words as when he equates '*Savanna*' with 'a plain open Piece of Meadow-Land' (p. 146). Moreover, he points to and establishes synonymy when he invites the reader to choose between such terms as flocks and herds (p. 163) and as anchor or grappling (p. 174). But, on the other hand, Crusoe is often lost for words. His inability to name strange wild animals makes them more fearful (p. 24) and that he cannot name a bird which he eats frustrates his need for order (p. 73). As narrator, he realizes that his inability to name his wandering impulse prevents him from analyzing it (p. 73) and that the impossibility of inventing a word for the unconventional leggings that he makes because they defy verbal and logical categories illustrates the barbarity of his situation on the island (p. 149). Like Moll, then, Crusoe is variously competent with language. He is not to be relied on for accuracy and insight in a uniform way. But Crusoe's very verbal inadequacies serve Defoe's thematic purposes.

As narrator Crusoe often confesses to being remote from his former experiences and unable to find words to describe them (e.g., pp. 11-12). Again, in recounting his rescue by the Portuguese captain (p. 33) and his relief at escaping drowning (p. 46), he can only stress the inexpressibility of his former feelings. Of course, there are occcasions—as, for instance, when he cannot detail his religious dream (p. 87) or elaborate upon the comforts that his musings about providence bring about (p. 130)—when Defoe makes Crusoe's sense of the ineffable support implicit religious ideas. But usually Crusoe's inability to express himself is used by Defoe to emphasize the point that, in addition to being necessary to religious sense, language must be recognized as significant only in society. Hence, through Crusoe's experience with words and names on the island Defoe wishes to educate the reader to an understanding of the conditions under which language best achieves sense. Certainly, Crusoe learns a lot about language on account of his isolation. Before he reaches the island he is proud of his own conversation (p. 17), but it is clear that, as in the case where he calls the promptings of his conscience 'Fits' (p. 10), he uses words to avoid moral responsibility. So, too, before his conversion his expressions of spiritual gratitude are merely formulaic and conventional. But, although the words of the Bible initially mean nothing to Crusoe, they still impress him and awaken in him a new sense of such words as deliverance. According to Defoe, this new sense of words is partly responsible for Crusoe's spiritual renewal (p. 97). But, despite his conversion and his attempts to be content with conversation with God, Crusoe suffers from his lack of human communication. No possible 'Energy of Words' can describe his longing for talk (p. 187). While, on account of this lack of communication, Crusoe comes to realize that language is instrumental to thought and action, through Crusoe's verbal usage Defoe implies the more precise and important theme that it is the social aspects of language which effect psychological security and moral control of nature.

In his solitary condition Crusoe uses words to compensate for his lack of society. Not only does he talk aloud to himself (p. 63) but, more significantly, he tries to dignify his merely private actions and thoughts with public words. He is particularly fond of political vocabulary. Hence, he frequently makes resolutions and once he even calls 'a Council, that is to say, in my Thoughts' (p. 54). The gap between the formality of his diction and the informality of his situation is striking, and the extension of meaning that he gives to many of his words is ironical. That, as narrator, he looks back sometimes with a cautious accuracy as regards changing names, as when, for example, he finds it possible to call his pale a wall and his hedge trees (pp. 67 and 105), serves to heighten those occasions when he varies his nouns without any authority or licence. Consider the time when he gratefully returns to his cave after his disturbing ramble across the island: he variously refers to his base as his 'old Hutch ... Place of Abode ... own Home ... perfect Settlement' (p. 111). The progression in denotation and connotation is unwarranted; it does, however, reveal Crusoe's need for society and value. His attempts to change things by giving them different names continually seem arbitrary and, therefore, indicate the social and conventional basis of usage and meaning. Hence, when he calls his 'Rags' 'Cloaths' and his 'Botching' 'Taylering' (p. 134), his verbal transformations are, in the slightest sense, nominal. The insecurity which the footprint establishes exaggerates Crusoe's tendency to transform his world by words which represent established, impressive, and public phenomena. Thus, his cave becomes his castle and his muskets become cannons (pp. 154 and 182). Interestingly, this verbal pretension does not stop when other people come to the island. So, despite the pleasure that he takes in Friday's voice (p. 204) and despite the ease which teaching Friday to speak English gives to Crusoe's life (p. 210), he still continues to create names in an arbitrary way. Consequently, he describes himself variously as a prince, a king, a head of state, and a general and governor. In his own eyes he possesses a family, subjects, and an army: he even lays claim to a commission of political authority over the island.[28] If we compare the way in which Crusoe appropriates public words to himself with the way in which Defoe, in *A Tour through the Whole Island of Great Britain*, uses the same terms to praise the Earl of Pembroke (vol. 1, p. 193), we shall see that, unlike the Earl, Crusoe is not comparable to a patriarchal monarch because he does not rule over the island with the authority that comes from moral discipline. Crusoe certainly aspires to the role which the Earl fulfills, but his aspirations merely show up his need for society, state, and political constitution. Through Crusoe's use of words, then, Defoe establishes verbal ironies and narrative contraries which question his character's attempt to recreate society and which promote commitment to society. Defoe clearly shows that many of Crusoe's words can be meaningful only as used in and by society. As it is, Crusoe's words do not achieve sense; they do not respect the fact that society is the vehicle for language and for the conversion of words into sense.

CHAPTER 5

The Uses of Narrative

> The Writer that strives to be useful, writes to *serve* you, and at the same Time, by an imperceptible Art, draws you on *to be pleased* also. He represents Truth with *Plainness*, Virtue with *Praise*, he even reprehends with a Softness that carries the Force of Satyr, without the Salt of it; and he insensibly screws himself so far into your good Opinion, that as his Writings merit your Regard, so they fail not to obtain it.[1]

There can be little doubt that, in addition to wanting his own writing to be useful and setting out in a self-consciously artful way to provide the reader of his narratives with pleasure, Defoe tried to develop the audience's implicit and inevitable reliance upon the writer in the hope that the necessary rhetorical strategies would form, as well as inform, his readers' understanding of his didactic purposes. It is possible to maintain, then, that, at the same time as he was committed to seizing fictional opportunities to promote political, social, and moral ideas, by involving his writings with implicit commentary upon the nature of narrative he was enabled to heighten these ideas. Of course, his strategic disposition of narrative must be seen partly in terms of his personal experience. Hence, when he recommended himself to Sir Robert Harley as a potential spy for the government, he boasted his ability to be all things to all men, and from his career as a polemical and controversial journalist he acquired a clear sense of the perpetual need to forestall criticism and to expend continuous energy in appealing to readers. But such personal factors are not as important in explaining his strategic use of narrative as the literary awareness that permitted him to move away from addressing particular or specialist audiences and to recognize that he could best give the general reader an ethical appreciation of contemporary issues by developing a moderate, comprehensive, and, therefore, authoritative point of view.[2]

A good explanation of his thoughts about the relation of point of view to the function of writing is to be found in his defence of the freedom of the press. For instance, he advanced the position that writing can stabilize society properly only if it is free from external political pressures and only if the writer's stance is absolved from immediate party political obligations. He regarded the Bible as the model of free expression because such writings as the maxims of Solomon and the story of Job apply to all the stations of life and provide general comfort before the vicissitudes of life. On the other hand, he attacked the contemporary prevalence of politically prejudiced accounts of writing and writers on the grounds that, in addition to authorial integrity, civil liberties, cultural development, and aesthetic discrimination were thereby being undermined. In Defoe's judgment, political prejudice threatened the general moral effectiveness of writing because it encouraged readers to think in terms not of an author's moral intentions and literary ability but of his political allegiance. The writer, Defoe thought, had to be allowed, for interdependent rhetorical and moral reasons, to generate a universal character and appeal for himself. In his own eyes he believed that he had achieved such authorial attributes. Indeed, he prided himself that his knowledge of the world and natural talents made him comparable to Shakespeare, and his complaisance, his good temper, and his endearing condescension, he also believed, lent his constant moral concerns a greater persuasiveness than those of scholars and clergymen and qualified him to be a protector of the true social purposes of writing.[3] It is not too difficult, however, to realize that this declaration of confidence in his own authoritative point of view is as much a matter of rhetorical emphasis as it is of personal conviction. Certainly, the declaration is not to be taken simply at face value, for it partly represents his appreciation of professional writing and his need to be esteemed as a gentleman and a writer. If, as a biographer claims, Defoe felt isolated by temperament and circumstance from the circles of polite literature, for persuasive reasons he did not necessarily admit this feeling. Even in the many works and perhaps most notably in *An Appeal to Honour and Justice* (1715), in which he laments his failure to affect audience and to match literary effect to intention, his confessions are not just personal statements. More often than not, they are rhetorical appeals for sympathy and agreement. Indeed, the rhetorical character of Defoe's statements about literary success and failure corresponds to his narrative stance. He usually avoids seeming eccentric or unrepresentative. Rather he makes himself and his spokesmen appear to be typical, normal, and broad-minded.[4] Because his concern with general cultural disorder committed him to the rhetorical function of literature and even to rhetorical descriptions of his own writing, he is not to be relied upon for systematic literary explanations.

That his apparent attempts to explain his point of view frequently turn out to be hortatory is testimony to Defoe's emphasis upon the uses of narrative. The same conclusion is to be deduced from various remarks he makes about the nature of his audience and of his literary task in confronting his readers.

These remarks tend to be quite relative and contrary. For instance, in *The Family Instructor* he announces that

> We live in an Age that does not want so much to know their Duty *as to practice it*, not so much *to be taught to know*, as to be made obedient to what they *already know*. (p. 2)

Confident in his knowledge of the prevailing ethos of his time, he suggests that, instead of moral instruction, people need exhortation. He sees his duty as a writer to be to close the gap between the established ethical sense and the unexercised moral will. But in *Serious Reflections* he describes his task as that of arousing people to knowledge of evil:

> It will be impossible to bring Vice out of Fashion, if we cannot bring Men to an Understanding of what it really is: But could we prevail upon a Man to examine his Vice, to dissect its Parts, and view the Anatomy of it; to see how disagreeable it is to him as a Man, as a Gentleman, or as a Christian; how despicable and contemptible in its highest Fruition; how destructive to his Senses, Estate, and Reputation; how dishonourable, and how beastly, in its publick Appearances, such a Man would certainly be out of Love with it, and be but Mankind once out of love with Vice, the Reformation is half brought to pass. (p. 87)

Here he asserts that people will stop being sinful if they are brought to understand evil through more comprehensive and categorical ways of thinking. He insists that, if people can be induced to think of themselves from multiple perspectives, they can be made to hate vice. In this case, then, Defoe believes his duty to be to bring people to moral knowledge by increasing their self-consciousness. These examples of his contrary estimates of the knowledge which his readers possess and of the effects which he wants to have on them cannot be rationalized by simply supposing that the audiences of the two works were different. For one thing, both estimates are expressed in general terms and in neither is Defoe's tone exclusive. For another, both estimates are rhetorical in that, even as they define requisite moral action, they encourage readers by means of compliments. In the first case, the audience's theoretical moral knowledge is implicitly praised, whereas, in the second, its capacity to actualize moral knowledge is stressed.

Another reason why the contrary estimates of the audience's needs cannot be rationalized is that they resemble the typically contrary way in which Defoe describes the effectiveness of narrative. In *Serious Reflections*, for example, he declares that a narrative which is obliged to move the reader's mind must incorporate facts that are 'done a great Way off, and by somebody never heard of' (p. xiii). But, elsewhere, he affirms that history and biography, precisely because they deal with well-known events and deservedly famous people, provide society with the best moral edification and are the most useful literary support to significant values and ideas.[5] In both instances, his concern is to promote the didactic function of literature, but his assumptions and the methods which he delineates are opposite. In the first, he proposes that a narrative which employs an unrecognizable setting and fictional characters will exert a most moving appeal, and, in the second, he argues that such an effect will be achieved only if narrative possesses relevance, an immediately recognizable setting, and real characters. These contrary presentations of the source of narrative effectiveness partly indicate Defoe's willingness to exploit basic narrative tensions for didactic purposes and his consequent unconcern with systematic literary theory. More evidence for this point can be gathered from the contrary way in which he connects narration to life. Hence, in *Serious Reflections*, in order to dignify *Robinson Crusoe*, he calls the latter an allusive, allegorical history of his own life and claims that it is reasonable 'to represent any Thing that really exists, by that which exists not' (p. xii), but later in the same work, when he comes to defend the ultimate value of revelation, he maintains that 'We can Form no Idea of any Thing that we know not and have not seen, but in the Form of something that we have seen' (p. 288). From these differing accounts of the limits of empirical ideas it appears that, at one and the same time, Defoe held that experience was and was not the source of ideas and the groundwork of representation and that narrative to the extent that it may be symbolic can be true to spiritual meaning while to the extent that it cannot take the place of revelation in the unfolding of spiritual meaning it is restricted to a mere transcription of sensuous experience. At one moment, therefore, he asserts that narrative is able to convey the most significant aspects of a person's interior life, but at the next he implies that, in contrast with revelation, narrative cannot transcend ordinary experience. Yet in neither passage is he intent on explaining his literary ideas systematically: he introduces them in the first one mainly to justify his writing and thereby to establish his own trustworthiness and in the second one to heighten by contrast the doctrine of religious grace. Clearly, he employs contrary literary ideas for ulterior and extraliterary reasons.

That Defoe's several comments on the nature of narrative are difficult to reconcile with one another because they are subordinated to local rhetorical effects suggests his interest in the various uses of narrative and shows that he was not mainly concerned with treating literary phenomena from a literary point of view. Even when, as in the epigraph to this chapter, he seems to present a conventional literary description of the writer's role, his sense of the multiple functions which the author should serve entails a heightening of the usual paradoxes. Although, that is, the epigraph is an expression of very ordinary literary theory in that it emphasizes the interdependent duties of the writer to teach and to delight, Defoe's articulation heightens the contraries involved in that theory. Hence, he requires a writer to be plain and covert, to serve directly and to gratify imperceptibly. In addition, he suggests that a good writer must be polite and forceful, must openly win the reader's good opinion yet must insinuate himself into that favour irresistibly. This especially paradoxical description of ideal authorial manner derives from Defoe's commitment to make literature useful in various ways and to reform, as well as to educate, his readers.[6]

One way in which Defoe uses narrative to reform his readers is to expose the vicarious gratification which narrative itself can stimulate. His accounts of pirates, for example, challenge the reader's desire for excitement and satirize the taste for adventure stories by exploiting tensions between fact and fiction. In *The King of Pirates* (1719) he concentrates upon removing the 'romantick, improbable, and impossible Parts' from Avery's life (p. vi). He rejects the legendary accretions to the story of this famous pirate by composing a fictional autobiography in which Avery himself is made to confess that his life is unworthy of romantic speculation and that much of his fame rests on a gross distortion of facts. In order, then, to discomfit readers who prefer the story of a pirate to conform to escapist notions of fictional adventure, Defoe creates a very different fictional image of Avery. By manipulating the pirate's account so that it substantiates his own editorial attack upon romance, Defoe implicitly justifies his fiction because it is truthful about Avery and romantic fiction. That he creates a fictional Avery to be a spokesman for such factual matters shows that he relies upon narrative as long as it is a means for deflating narrative which is appreciated as an end in itself. Furthermore, by establishing the illusion that Avery, from some distance in time and space, attacks the English preference for exotic adventure stories, Defoe testifies to his concern to impress his audience with actual, local issues. That is, the fiction that the infamous outlaw disapproves of the fictional respect that he is given and shares his creator's domestic values demonstrates Defoe's subtlety about narrative reinforcement of his real point of view. His account of Avery in *A General History of the Pyrates* (1724) exploits narrative in a similarly contrary way. For, to scotch the rumour that Avery had become the king of Madagascar, Defoe insists that, at the very time when he was supposed to have attained such romantic eminence, the pirate, having been ignominiously cheated out of his remaining wealth by Bristol merchants, had died an obscure beggar in the north Devon town of Bideford (pp. 25-36). That there is no evidence for this story again exemplifies the way in which Defoe employs narrative for rhetorical effect and his readiness to treat historical figures with fictional licence as long as by so doing he can deflate merely fanciful imaginings and assert social realities.[7]

On account of his wish to encourage readers to develop an appreciation of fiction that is related to a moral understanding of social realities, Defoe adopts several narrative attitudes towards pirates in *A General History of the Pyrates*. Although, most commonly, he presents them as a 'Parcel of Robbers' (A4v) because he refuses to make them into objects of fictional admiration, he expresses more than dismissive sentiments about them. For instance, he blames society for the prevalence of pirates: he considers it society's fault that projects for the relief of unemployed seamen have not been implemented (A2v). His proposal that a national fishery would reduce the number of pirates reveals how close the impulse of this narrative is to that of *An Essay upon Projects*. Moreover, that he should attribute the prevalence of pirates to the scepticism and infidelity of the age and to the corrupting influence of *'Polite Literature'*[8] shows that what sympathy he has for them is relative to the sense of the need for reformation which the Revolution of 1688 had inspired in him (pp. 81-83). Indeed, for the purpose of goading his readers into an appreciation of this need, he presents one pirate, Captain North, favourably. The latter is praised for being more humane than the average member of society who, according to Defoe, is not concerned enough about the injustices and cruelties of debtors' prisons. Further insight into his readiness to incorporate social projecting into his account of the pirates comes from the recognition that he invented the entirely fictional Captain Mission to create the illusion that this outsider can observe the faults of European politics and religion and with the authority of abstract reasoning can call for major reforms.[9] If, however, Defoe endows some of the pirates with authentically critical ideas for his own social purposes, he is careful to disclaim the deistic and utopian notions that he gives to other pirates. His intention to imply the theme of social contentment leads him to make many of the pirates long for their homes, for instance. By employing the theme of primitivism on the occasion when he praises the moral sense of the Calabar negroes for refusing to trade with pirates (p. 199), his standing aloof from the pirates enables him to criticize European morality. This occasion represents another example of his willingness to tolerate motifs with which he had no ideological sympathy as long as they could serve as a means to oblige his readers to think of fiction in a more socially responsible way.

Of course, his commitment to the Revolution settlement sometimes caused him to be unconcerned about narrative coherence. That he could exploit narrative in the simplest of ways for reasons of propaganda is seen nowhere better perhaps than in *Madagascar: or, Robert Drury's Journal*. Although Drury was a real person whom Defoe met and with whom he discussed his adventures and although Defoe claimed to be merely the transcriber and editor of Drury's book, the interesting aspects of the account are not historical. In the preface Defoe confesses to having improved the religious and political aspects of the account because he could not resist applying them properly. But what constitutes a proper application to Defoe happens to be at odds with Drury's narrative. For his criticism of Hobbes's conception of the state of nature in the preface is not at all substantiated by Drury's account, since the latter shows that the people of Madagascar are in a perpetual state of war, and the sermon in which he makes Drury draw parallels between the origins of government in Madagascar and England is defied by the facts of the narrative. Defoe interpolates the sermon simply to make his readers accept the constitution: through Drury he insists that, despite the economic specialization and the social hierarchy which conceal the egalitarian bases of society, the constitution affords equal rights to all since it is founded on reason and nature (pp. 153-55). Certainly, Defoe must have valued the general appeal of Drury's account, but his propaganda does not respect its narrative integrity.

But Defoe did know that the composition of narrative should be an arduous moral activity and he usually exerted himself in that direction when narrating the lives of historical personages. A comparison of *The Life of Jonathan Wild* (1725) and *The True and Genuine Account of Jonathan Wild* (1725) illustrates his understanding that the effectiveness of narrative depends largely on the moral character of the narrator.[10] He makes the narrators of these accounts of the infamous gangster quite different. The narrator of the first is H.D., once a clerk to Justice Raymond before whom Wild was tried, while the narrator of the second is an earnest and somewhat austere professional writer. The clerk professes to be committed to accuracy of detail and so justifies to himself his reliance upon the thief-taker's own words. But he is vicariously attracted by both Wild's vanity and his cunning manipulation of society. Interestingly, the clerk's social perspective is confused because, although he relishes the anti-social nature of Wild's conduct of his criminal affairs and management of his gang, he describes these things as social achievements. For example, the clerk's admiration of Wild's 'System of Politicks' makes him esteem the criminal for being as worthy as a statesman (p. vi). To a certain extent it is possible that such ironical flattery might demonstrate that the clerk's account conforms to the contemporary allegorization of Wild's life which had come about from a desire to mount a political opposition to Sir Robert Walpole. But, when contrasted with the more general political commentary of the second account, it seems plain that Defoe's sustained satire is directed against the clerk himself and the legalistic notion of morality that he stands for. On the other hand, the responsible author begins his account by condemning both Wild and those who find him cause for entertainment. To him, Wild is an *'infamous Creature'* and those who are *'so fond of a formal Chimney-corner Tale, that they had rather a Story should be merry than true'* are repugnant. Intent upon exercising a consistent moral viewpoint, the author discounts Wild's perspective, attacks the commercial exploitation of criminal biographies, and, without pretending to prize verisimilitude, insists upon the thoroughness of research that has gone into his account.

Clearly, Defoe implies that, because the clerk enjoys describing Wild's antisocial behaviour comically, his narrative stance is ineffective as well as immoral. Certainly, that it is merely episodic and lacks a rational structure is due mostly to the clerk's self-satisfaction with offering a random selection of Wild's rogueries. By regarding the criminal as a laudable businessman and being gratified by the thief-taker's success at maintaining the respect of those whom he defrauds, the clerk reveals that, despite his legal experience, he has no sense of the need for the reform of the law and society. His celebration of Wild's ability to exploit the vulnerability of the poor and to blackmail them into becoming criminals to serve his interest exemplifies the clerk's unawareness of his inevitable alienation of the reader. The clerk does not know how he diminishes his rhetorical appeal by pretending to be at one with Wild. Again, the shortcomings of his narrative stance are evidenced when, after describing the law that was passed against the receiving of stolen goods, his attitude towards Wild abruptly changes and he condemns him for a lack of prudence in ignoring the law. It is not surprising that the clerk should supply a merely conventional comment when he describes Wild's death. By contrast, the author's narrative stance is effective because it is factual, coherent, and moral. He does not just focus on Wild. Instead, he sees matters in a connected way. Hence, in addition to depreciating Wild's opportunistic exploitation of poor criminals, he argues that the deficiencies of the public administration and of public attitudes permitted the thief-taker to abuse the poor and to plunder society. His strong awareness of the general good prompts him to condemn those people who were so taken up with self-interest that, after recovering their stolen belongings from Wild, they still believed him to be honest. He also attributes Wild's success not to skill but to the government's naive attempts to rid the land of criminals. The author is disgusted that Wild could satisfy the government with a steady flow of victims for the law at the same time as he was training more criminals for his illegal enterprises. He is even more disgusted that nothing was done to prevent Wild from turning disadvantaged children into hardened criminals. The consistency of the author's satire together with his constantly humanitarian perspective on the relation of the individual and society ensures that no conventional moral tag is to be found at the end of his account.

In his narrative stance the author criticizes just those aspects of society and fiction which in his account the clerk embraces. That is, the clerk congratulates himself on his acquaintanceship with Wild and proudly thinks that this entitles him to respect from his readers. His equal complacency in life and literature shows that his real desire in writing is to be *'himself the Heroe of his own Romance.'*[11] This sort of emotional gratification does not hamper the professional author. He maintains a steady social perspective and refuses to treat Wild simply as an individual. The composition of the criminal biography is a conscious moral activity which entails for him self-discipline. The author's differences from the clerk reveal Defoe's appreciation of the strategies of narrative and manifest his sense of the social usefulness of biography.

Despite his sense of the writer's serious responsibility in the handling of historical figures, Defoe still believed that he could reform readers by composing fictional criminal autobiographies. His awareness that 'A TALE *may please him whom a Sermon flies*'[12] prompted him to exploit this literary kind and to use the distinct narrative manners which the clerk and the professional author embody in their different treatments of Jonathan Wild. In *Street-Robberies, Consider'd* (1728), for example, Defoe employs one narrative mode to teach and another to delight. The narrator of this supposed tale is a converted thief who, after twenty years of respectable living and repentance for his former crimes, writes to let society benefit from his various experiences. Both the *exemplum* and the spokesman for Defoe's views on society, the narrator speaks in two different ways: as narrator he does not possess a consistent character. He recounts his criminal origins in a vulgar, amusing, and picaresque manner. The enjoyment he wins from telling about his early life is conveyed by mock-heroic diction and by a comically absurd sense of detachment from the past. This narrative voice, far from reflecting a penitent mind, seems both unrealistic and unfeeling. Yet in his other voice the narrator speaks with feeling about his former self and about the projects for the reformation of society which both his criminal and moral life have led him to define. An insight into this deliberate narrative inconsistency can be gained from considering two motifs which *Street-Robberies, Consider'd* has in common with *Colonel Jack* (1723). As with Colonel Jack, the narrator's first robbery is of a helpless fruit-woman whose likely destitution spurs him to self-incrimination and restitution. Again like Colonel Jack, the narrator tells of how he twice learned to read and write.[13] Such incidental motifs show Defoe's desire to heighten the plaintive lot of the poor and, at the same time, to encourage their conscientiousness and social usefulness. The concerned voice, which Defoe gives to the narrator in order to promote his views about the essential willingness of criminals and the poor to be productive members of society, is manifest in the narrator's projects for social reform many of which correspond to the ones Defoe proposes in *Augusta Triumphans* (1728). Similarly to his creator in this tract, the narrator of *Street-Robberies, Consider'd* attacks *The Beggar's Opera* for making light of criminality, indicates the need for fuller employment of the poor and for the spiritual instruction of prisoners, and argues that robberies will be reduced only if the Watch is improved (pp. 50-59). By juxtaposing picaresque and doctrinaire voices in the narrative Defoe no doubt thought that he could reach a different audience from that which would read the more consistent and yet more abstract *Augusta Triumphans*. Since, however, Defoe's ideas for social reform committed him to a mixture of satire and exhortation, as an agent of this double literary aim the converted robber's rhetorical appeal is ambivalent and to this extent he is merely a device to establish his creator's themes.

Defoe's preference for employing narrative to comment on social issues is evident in his biographies of eminent people, for in these works he still tends to use the central figures as vehicles for the restatement of his arguments on behalf of the constitution and moral reformation. The biographies certainly do not concentrate upon making their well known subjects exemplary simply as individuals: their narrative stance is usually public rather than intimate. In *Memoirs of Daniel Williams* (1718), for instance, Defoe describes nothing of his subject's personal or domestic life. Instead, he focusses upon William's dedicated work for the Dissenters. For long stretches of the narrative, however, Williams remains in the background while Defoe recounts the history of Dissent after the Revolution. What he seems to value most in the writing of this biography is the opportunity to repeat his critical analysis of the moral harm done to the Dissenters' cause by occasional conformity and by moves, as in the case of the Test Act, to abolish political restrictions on the religious community. Inasmuch as Williams is eulogized for organizing an administration of church funds, for improving the training of ministers, and for regularizing the dissenting academies, he is celebrated as an agent of reform and for amending those faults which Defoe had catalogued earlier in, for example, *The Present State of the Parties in Great Britain* (1712, p. 291 ff). Undoubtedly, Defoe uses biography as a form that allows him to continue addressing the problems with which he had been concerned for years.

In *Some Account of the Life of Sir Charles Sedley* (1721) again there is little emphasis on biography as an end in itself. For, even though Defoe praises Sedley's work it is not just with the intention of promoting his poetry. He appreciates Sedley as a means of depreciating the more famous Restoration poets. Moreover, in order to criticize the ethos of Charles II's court, he is quite prepared to emphasize the corruption of Sedley's morals (p. 7). Defoe clearly uses this biography to reaffirm the sense of history which the Revolution conveyed to him. What, indeed, most appeals to him about Sedley is the latter's commitment to the Revolution settlement: 'At the Revolution, he appeared warm on the Side of King *William*; and particularly, he stickl'd hard for Voting the Throne vacant, as also, for Filling it up.' It is obvious that Sedley's radical interest in constitutional reform and his disgust with Stuart immorality weigh heavier than his literary achievements in Defoe's judgment.

Defoe's method of looking beyond the subjects of his biographies as a way of illustrating more abstract concerns is easily traced in *Mere Natured Delineated*. Although this work offers to focus upon Peter the wild boy who, having been found in a forest in Hanover, had been brought to England as an example of a noble savage, Defoe's belief in the irrelevance of primitivistic thinking and his deliberate narrative flexibility encourage the reader to view the work as a mock biography which serves important satire. Indeed, Defoe treats Peter in contrary ways for ironical purposes: he never regards him straightforwardly as an individual who is a legitimate object of inquiry. Peter is a device by which the narrative can decry the political and social decadence of the upper classes. In addition, however, to helping Defoe to satirize polite society, Peter provides the means by which the narrative can implicitly support certain positive social attitudes. Although Defoe conveys his views about primitivistic theory early on by forthrightly attacking contemporary courtiers as 'the beauteous shadows of a Nothing' (p. 2), he soon becomes more subtle in his satirical strategy. For instance, he deliberately varies his emotional stance towards Peter and society. He can be quite unsympathetic to Peter as a way of promoting commitment to society. Hence, he reports Peter's inability to respond positively to English society and deduces, assuming momentarily that this society is sound, that such a response can only mean that Peter lacks a soul. Next, by analogy, he contends that those English people who do not value their society must also lack souls. On the other hand, he can similarly exploit apparent sympathy for Peter. So, when he considers Peter's thoughtless state another time, he resists judging the wild boy by pretending to be reluctant to accept the orthodox belief that the soul is the agent of thought. But the cause of this reluctance is not a feeling for the wild boy. Rather it is a sense of irony. For he goes on to pretend not to want to admit the corollary of the orthodox belief, namely, that all those who do not think do not possess souls, because this corollary would oblige him to condemn the whole of polite society (p. 19)! Clearly, his ambivalent stance towards Peter enables Defoe to deflate natural perspectives on society and to insinuate the necessity of reform according to orthodox religious standards. Hence, Defoe converts the narrative assertion that Peter has the habit of laughing without knowing why into an analogy of the ridiculers of the age whose naturalistic tenets demonstrate that they have reduced themselves to a mere state of nature. That, furthermore, Defoe can affirm at one moment that Peter wishes to leave the court, even though speculators there have granted him possession of a soul, and at another time that he is mindlessly happy at court because of his proximity to naturally sympathetic people is evidence of his contrary stance performing a unified satirical function. Whether or not Peter is happy at court and whether or not he has moral integrity, Defoe still establishes his view about the lack of civilization and morality at court. By means, then, of ironical narrative contraries in the presentation of Peter, Defoe uses biography to explode natural morality and to argue implicitly the court's obligation to be concerned about society and the constitution in orthodox ways.

Of particular significance for an understanding of how Defoe used narrative is his composition of fictional military memoirs. In varying degrees these works employ a narrator to assert political and moral ideas which Defoe had previously articulated in more obviously didactic terms. These works, in the main, uphold the Revolution settlement, promote an aggressive foreign policy, decry the interference of party politics in military affairs, and, by means of eulogizing actual military heroes, suggest the reasons why society should respect military virtues. The consequence of this emphasis on political themes is that the character of the narrator is not presented as more than a rhetorical function. Certainly, for strategical and persuasive reasons Defoe does, to some extent, create the illusion that the narrators have experienced the facts and ideas which they relate, but the ideological causes which the narrators serve are so transparent and dominant that as images of real people they are necessarily inadequate. Consider, for example, the anonymous officer who is Defoe's persona in *An Apology for the Army* (1715). The officer's real purpose is to chastise the Tories for opposing foreign policy and to argue that their avoidance of military conflict is a subversion of public morality. His specific object of derision is the attempt of Bolingbroke and others to conclude a treaty with France which would have restored the Pretender without consultation with the Protestant Allies. Outraged by the consideration that the Tories had sought to betray the country, the constitution, and Protestantism, the officer charges that, as a way of concealing this betrayal, the Tories had also endeavoured to degrade the image of the army in the minds of the populace. His task is to refurbish this image by defining the nature of military fortitude and by maintaining that military heroism represents the type of selfless concern for the public good which is necessary for both national security and the protection of individual rights. To exemplify military heroism the officer recalls the career of the Duke of Argyle. But, at the same time as he praises this military leader, the officer reminds his readers of the way in which the Tory government had abused the Duke by sending him to fight in Spain without sufficient provisions even as it was bargaining for peace (p. 37). By having his narrator celebrate a military leader who had been hostile to the Jacobite cause and instrumental in securing the Hanoverian succession[14] and by making the officer end his apology with a direct appeal to George I's administration to treat the army with greater respect, Defoe demonstrably employs narrative to convey his faith in the Revolution settlement. If it is clear, however, that the officer's ideas are more important than his character, Defoe does imply that his narrator's rational, sensible, and concerned stance is a concomitant of these ideas.

The purpose of *The Memoirs of Majr. Alexander Ramkins* (1718) is also to defend the Hanoverian succession and to deflate Jacobitism. In this military memoir Defoe's major fiction is the creation of a narrator who was once an ardent Jacobite but who has become a firm supporter of the Protestant constitution. Ramkins's memoirs, nevertheless, are personal only in the limited sense that they are concerned with political creed. Hence, his account is taken up mostly with relating his supposedly direct experience of Louis XIV's attitude to James II's cause and with explaining how the lessons of history, as well as his own political experience, have persuaded him to stop being a Jacobite. Although he gives an air of authenticity to Ramkins's exposure of French political strategy by making his narrator seem authoritative, objective, and personable, Defoe spends considerably more effort in arranging that Ramkins's commentary is directed towards undermining Jacobite prejudices in favour of the French. Consequently, Ramkins reiterates Defoe's own view that French support for Jacobitism was merely a political strategy to distract England from interfering with France's imperial pretensions. To discountenance Jacobite idealism Ramkins is also made to stress that France never joined war with England from a sense of religious obligation to re-establish James II. When, towards the end of his account, Ramkins confesses that he has disowned the prejudices that had made him a Jacobite, he rejects the significance of the doctrines of hereditary right and of the divine right of kings. That he can so easily overturn fundamental Jacobite beliefs in order to acknowledge the Revolution settlement and to accept with gratitude the benefits which derive from the constitution's indulgence of Catholics reveals precisely the sort of rhetorical appeal that Defoe embodied in his narrator. Since Ramkins feels comfortable about being a Catholic in a Protestant constitution and since he opposes the Hanoverian succession neither in conscience nor in policy, Defoe can be seen to be using Ramkins's purported political conversations as a device with which to comprehend Jacobites within the *status quo*. Ramkins the narrator testifies, then, once again to Defoe's belief that the passing years were justifying the Revolution and William's policies and to his rhetorical stance that this was obvious to anyone with a sense of impartiality and truth.

Defoe's desire to justify the Revolution from as broad an historical perspective as possible underlies his composition of *The Memoirs of an English Officer* (1728). Although in this work, as is typical, Defoe is not concerned about presenting the officer's personal experience or thoughts, he does use the officer as a device to provide a survey of the important events of the Dutch War, the Seven Years War, and the War of Spanish Succession and invites the reader to deduce from the survey that the officer is experienced in fighting for the national good and to respect the historical basis of his knowledge. It is revealing that the largest proportion of the survey is given over to a rehearsal of the Earl of Peterborough's struggles to wage a serious campaign in Spain despite Tory political machinations. No doubt, the fact that Peterborough had been one of the first men of rank to encourage William to try for the crown of England[15] must have disposed Defoe to revere his memory. Certainly, one of the major functions of this narrative is to praise Peterborough's courage, military ingenuity, and personal prowess and to attribute his successes to a faith in the Revolution. On the other hand, the narrative blames the eventual failure of the war in Spain upon the Tory government's dismissal of Peterborough (p. 201). The officer is unhesitating in condemning the dismissal of such a hero as a deliberate attempt to reject William's foreign policy and the Revolution settlement. While, then, the English officer records nothing of heroic proportions about his own actions, his function seems to be to provide an illusion of the immediate and overwhelming heroism of Peterborough. As a helpful and intelligent confidant of the general, the English officer is enabled to convey a sense of Peterborough's humanity and principles. But, as the account progresses, the officer's function changes slightly and his articulation of his creator's concerns becomes somewhat more obvious. Hence, at the end of the war and before returning home the officer journeys through

Spain developing a critical sense of Catholic superstition and an appreciation for landscape and gardening: the style of his observations on these matters is very close to Defoe's. More importantly, however, the officer's relaxation in Spain is used to heighten the disgust with rampant political factionalism which he discovers on his return home (p. 350). His comments on the harmful effects upon society which excessive political partisanship incurs and his remarks about the necessity of reconciliation are very similar in substance and tone to the views which Defoe had earlier expressed through the persona of Andrew Moreton in the preface to *The Protestant Monastery* (1726). That the officer, like Moreton, should be shocked into passivity by the factionalism and yet urge political action to overcome it shows that Defoe employed similar narrative contraries to heighten his arguments and exhortations in fictional and non-fictional works and that generic distinctions meant little to him in comparison with his constant thematic preoccupation.

Memoirs of a Cavalier (1720) is the most accomplished of Defoe's fictional military autobiographies: its exploitation of narrative contraries and subtle embodiment of ideological commitment illustrate how refined its author's didacticism could be. The preface elaborately pretends that the memoirs were composed much more than twenty years before publication since Defoe wanted to create the impression that they are informed by a distinctive and reliable historical perspective. But there is evidence that Defoe wrote the account more to devise a rhetorical appeal to his contemporaries than to divert them simply with a pseudo-historical character. One piece of evidence is that, after asserting that there is much circumstantial proof of the Cavalier's existence, he insists that there is no means of verifying the Cavalier's identity. Indeed, he wishes 'to terminate the Enquiry after the Person.'[16] More evidence that he wanted to use the narrative for purposes beyond the creation of the Cavalier's viewpoint comes in the typically contrary dictates that the memoirs are authentic because they conform to standard histories of the Civil War and that they confute the 'many Errors in all the Writers upon the Subject of our Wars in *England*' (p. 3). To a certain extent, his recommendation of the accuracy and aesthetic pleasures of the memoirs betokens Defoe's actual manipulation of the narrator for the purpose of rewriting history from the moral perspective of the Revolution. The putative literary skills of the Cavalier are less evidence of Defoe's interest in his character than they are a sign of Defoe's ingenuity in generating implicit persuasion. By making the naive young royalist develop a political sense that his cause cannot match and by showing that, after an exposure to the complex political repercussions of the Civil War, the Cavalier comes to value the constitution in an independent, self-taught way, Defoe tries to create the illusion that the Cavalier had anticipated the political sense which the Revolution incorporated.

During the course of the narrative Defoe gradually educates the Cavalier in political knowledge so that, despite his youth and thoughtlessness, he is exposed to facts and problems which Defoe had reacted to in his earlier works. For example, in his travels through France, the Cavalier is informed about the English betrayal of the Huguenots of Rochelle: he learns enough to concede the fact and to ponder the need for a Protestant alliance in Europe (pp. 15-16). His views of this issue repeat, if somewhat more vaguely, Defoe's commentary in such works as *Lex Talionis*. But, by endowing the character of the Cavalier with contraries, Defoe establishes political implications despite the character. Hence, when the Cavalier admits that 'an Aversion of popular Tumults' prompted him to be a royalist at the same time as he contrasts the French monarchy's ability to use political compromise to quell public disorder with Charles I's failure in 'the Management of Politicks' (p. 21), ironically he justifies the advent of the Civil War and sheds doubt on his own royalist principles. At one moment, then, the narrative emphasizes the Cavalier's good sense and willingness to learn while, at the next, it calls attention to his shortsightedness: but both stances further the political themes. Of course, by so using contraries, Defoe can make the Cavalier's frequently sound judgment seem all the more sound precisely because it is natural and inconsistent. That, for instance, his supposed experience of the concatenation of mistakes and misperceptions that are involved in wars and treaties leads him to be intelligently critical of military life yet does not stop him from being an enthusiastic soldier testifies that, despite his ulterior purposes, Defoe deliberately gives the Cavalier life-like traits. Indeed, these traits, to the extent that they establish the Cavalier's rhetorical effectiveness, actually serve Defoe's ulterior purposes.

Since he is a very fallible individual, the Cavalier is not presented as a paradigm. But one way in which the Cavalier noticeably resembles his creator is in his celebration of heroes. Although Defoe affords his readers some fictional gratification by making the Cavalier a confidant of the King of Sweden, Charles I, and General Fairfax, the Cavalier's sense of heroism has the same force as Defoe's constant eulogies of King William. Through his supposed experience of Gustavus Adolphus's military campaign, the Cavalier arrives at a sense of society's and the individual's need for outstanding examples and heroic models. The King of Sweden is such a paradigm because, in addition to being perpetually accessible to his subjects and cultivating his own self-discipline as a way of encouraging regularity and order in society, his energy and spirit inspire religious reverence. Indeed,

Defoe obliges the Cavalier to confess that the brave deeds which he performs are the consequence of Adolphus's influence. By contrast, although he both likes Charles I as a person and feels committed to the royalist cause, the Cavalier admits to having been possessed of a lethargy because of the Stuart king's lack of spiritual energy. He feels, on the other hand, that, despite Fairfax's politics, the general was radiant with exemplary power and humanity: 'No Man in the World had more Fire and Fury in him while in Action, or more Temper and Softness out of it' (p. 265).

Through the figure of the Cavalier Defoe furnishes evidence of his belief in society's need for inspiring leadership and for a mixed constitution. Hence, when the Cavalier loses his initial enthusiasm for the Civil War, Defoe indicates that the deficiency is as much a public as a private one. Indeed, by emphasizing the Cavalier's personal faults, namely, his lack of religious principle and his hardened temper, Defoe heightens the significance of the Cavalier's disgust with the disorder of the army and the state. For, that the Cavalier can understand the public effects of the poor influence which Charles I exercises in society and can repeatedly lament the King's subjection to religious and political interests reveals Defoe's desire to validate his character's latent sense of political constitution. Furthermore, by employing narrative contraries Defoe continually shows that in his failures and successes the Cavalier exemplifies society's need for a balanced constitution. So, even as his responsibilities and authority grow, he is affected by the malaise and lack of corporate sense which derive from the weakness of the King's role and the failure of social order. As a result, he cannot always motivate his troops in a reasoned way and sometimes he commits unsoldierly acts (p. 256). Despite his potential for greatness, his energy, and his efficiency, because of the pervading disorder and public unconcern for constitutional matters, the Cavalier cannot connect his actions to his will, cannot, that is, perform heroic deeds. Nor, for the same reason, can he avoid making contrary statements. At one moment, shocked by the brutality of the war into lethargy, he has no resources to enable him to observe and to comment: 'a strange secret and unaccountable Sadness' falls upon his spirits (p. 165). But the narrative insists that at the next moment he could judge that the conduct of the war on both sides was conducted with humanity (p. 168). To a considerable extent, the uncertainties and inconsistencies of the Cavalier reflect his reaction to cultural and political chaos, while his latent virtues demonstrate that individuals will not develop morally unless they possess firm ideas about the state and nationality. That he is glad that Charles's ministers were purged by Parliament while he is angry that it assumed royal prerogatives reveals an emotional variability which betokens not so much personal consistency as a political sense of the need for a mixed constitution. His ability to recognize the harmful religious sectarianism in both the royalist and parliament sides is evidence of Defoe's wish to make the Cavalier seem impartial and balanced. Certainly, the Cavalier does propose constructive political ideas at the end of his account. For example, he argues for the removal of factional and sectarian strife from government and he defends the rights of both the monarchy and Parliament. In both his negative and positive statements the Cavalier seems to imply consistently the necessity of a mixed constitution (p. 271). The Cavalier's innate sense of the constitution as the basis of value and of the structures of daily life is one of the best examples of the subtlety with which Defoe could use narration and narrative dialectic for the rhetorical transposition of his own values and ideas.

Defoe's strategic uses of narrative prove that in his own mind he subordinated realistic techniques to didactic purposes and that, despite the feeling that his fiction is escapist, he intended his narratives to provoke reflections about basic, abstract issues in the contemporary situation. Both his application of distant temporal and spatial settings and his dialectical method of characterization testify to his desire to confront the reader with problems which he thought were vitally current and to exemplify moral ideas about society. Because he founded plot so consistently on the tension between actualities and possibilities, he can be seen to subordinate character to theme and to wish to prevent people from reading his narratives as if they are merely fictitious. Indeed, by depriving the reader of a stable fictional illusion, Defoe expected his narrative flexibility and variability to make his didacticism more efficient. The implicit calculating presence of Defoe in most of his narratives makes it difficult to accept that there is a problematic relation between the artist and the moralist in his actual writing. Granted, he did lie about the authenticity of his narratives and he did condemn himself when he insisted that an author who told one lie to correct another furthered, rather than remedied, moral corruption. But he was not interested in literary theory except in so far as it helped him to achieve rhetorical effects. Certainly, he preferred not to be systematic about the writer's role. If he holds up, for instance, a priestly model to the writer, he also insists that the writer must go beyond the limits of priestly decorum in the reproving of vice. By embodying dialectical notions both in his statements about writing and in his narratives themselves Defoe provides evidence that he did not consider himself to be committed to presenting in his fiction either an adversary culture or psychological realism. He saw his task as the stabilization and refinement of society, and in his narratives he disposes his themes in ways which show that they are clearly, if indirectly and variously, related to his social ideas.[17]

NOTES

For the convenience of the reader, references in this study have been made to modern or relatively accessible editions. But, in cases where references are given to other than original editions, actual citations follow the first editions.

NOTES TO THE PREFACE

[1] Defoe, *A System of Magick* (London, 1726), p. 117.
[2] Maximillian E. Novak, *Defoe And The Nature Of Man* (London, 1963), p. 8.
[3] James Sutherland, *Daniel Defoe: A Critical Study* (Boston, 1971), p. 41 and Novak, *Defoe And The Nature Of Man*, p. 21.
[4] Peter Earle, *The World Of Defoe* (London, 1976), pp. 29-32.

NOTES TO CHAPTER ONE

[1] Defoe, *Applebee's Journal* for March 18, 1721 in William Lee, *Daniel Defoe: His Life and Recently Discovered Writings: Extending from 1716 to 1729* (London, 1869), II, p. 353.
[2] *The Storm* (London, 1704), pp. 1-10.
[3] *Serious Reflections During The Life and Strange Adventures of Robinson Crusoe*, ed. G. H. Maynadier (Boston, 1903), p. 82.
[4] *A General History of Discoveries and Improvements* (London, 1725-1726), p. 238.
[5] *An Enquiry into the Case of Mr. Asgil's General Translation* (London, 1703), pp. 10-11.
[6] *Ibid*, p. 10.
[7] *The Storm*, p. 4. Defoe also considered Bacon an authority on mental culture: see *A Collection of Miscellany Letters, Selected out of Mist's Weekly Journal. The Fourth Volume* (London, 1727), p. 194.
[8] *A General History of Discoveries*, p. 232.
[9] Bacon, *The New Atlantis* in *The Philosophical Works of Francis Bacon*, ed. John M. Robertson (London, 1905), p. 717. See also Basil Willey, *The English Moralists* (London, 1964), p. 125 and *The Storm*, p. 9.
[10] Bacon, *The Advancement of Learning* in *The Philosophical Works*, pp. 44-45.
[11] *A General History of Discoveries*, pp. 219-22.
[12] *The Consolidator* in Henry Morley, *The Earlier Life and The Chief Earlier Works of Daniel Defoe* (London, 1889), p. 280.
[13] *An Enquiry into the Case of Mr. Asgil's General Translation*, p. 8.

[14] *A Collection of Miscellany Letters. Selected out of Mist's Weekly Journal. The Second Volume* (London, 1722), p. 124.
[15] *Ibid*, p. 113.
[16] *Ibid*, p. 126.
[17] *Ibid*, p. 127.
[18] *The Political History of the Devil* in *The Novels and Miscellaneous Works of Daniel De Foe*, ed. Sir Walter Scott (London, 1887), III, p. 471 and *A Tour through the Whole Island of Great Britain*, ed. G. D. H. Cole and D. C. Browning (London, 1974), I, p. 63.
[19] *Conjugal Lewdness: Or, Matrimonial Whoredom* (London, 1727), p. 131: in the course of an attack on unreproductive sexual indulgence Defoe cites Browne's pejorative application of the word 'coition' in order to stress that man's animal nature needs to be tempered by religious moderation. See *Religio Medici* in *Religio Medici and Other Works*, ed. L. C. Martin (Oxford, 1964), p. 67.
[20] See Leonard Nathanson, *The Strategy of Truth: A Study of Sir Thomas Browne* (Chicago, 1967), p. 116 and *Religio Medici*, pp. 4 and 26.
[21] *The Christianity of the High-church Consider'd* (London, 1704), p. 17.
[22] *The Life And Strange Surprizing Adventures Of Robinson Crusoe*, ed. J. Donald Crowley (London, 1976), p. 221.
[23] See *Religio Medici*, part two, section nine.
[24] *An Essay upon Literature* (London, 1726), pp. 35-37.
[25] *Review* III, p. 415.
[26] *The Storm*, p. 4.
[27] *The Consolidator*, pp. 306-08.
[28] See Richard Peters, *Hobbes* (London, 1967), pp. 129-77.
[29] *The Fortunes And Misfortunes Of the Famous Moll Flanders*, ed. G. A. Starr (London, 1976), p. 98.
[30] *Serious Reflections*, p. 10.
[31] *Moll Flanders*, pp. 281 and 287.
[32] *A Short Narrative of the Life and Actions of His Grace John, D. of Marlborough* (London, 1711), p. 4.
[33] *The Wickedness of a Disregard to Oaths* (1723), p. 6. There is no certainty that Defoe wrote this piece, although judging from content and style there is every probability that he did. See John Robert Moore, *A Checklist of the Writings of Daniel Defoe* (Hampden, Connecticut, 1971), pp. 184-85.
[34] *Robinson Crusoe*, pp. 209-10.
[35] *Madagascar: or, Robert Drury's Journal* (London, 1729), pp. xi-xiv.
[6] *Jure Divino*, Bk III, pp. 4-7.
[7] *Persecution Anatomiz'd* (London, 1725), pp. 2-5 and 13.

[36] *Moll Flanders*, pp. 173-74.
[37] *Robinson Crusoe*, pp. 156 and 188.
[38] *The Farther Adventures of Robinson Crusoe* (London, 1719), pp. 187 and 3.
[39] *Serious Reflections*, pp. 4-9.
[40] Lee, *Daniel Defoe*, II, pp. 348-50.
[41] Lee, *Daniel Defoe*, II, pp. 408-09; *A Collection of Miscellany Letters. The Fourth Volume*, p. 63; *A Collection of Miscellany Letters, Selected out of Mist's Weekly Journal. The Third Volume* (London, 1727), p. 185.
[42] Lee, *Daniel Defoe*, III, pp. 344-51.
[43] *The Commentator* of Monday 8th February, 1720.
[44] *Mercurius Politicus* of August, 1718, pp. 442 and 447.
[45] Lee, *Daniel Defoe*, III, p. 133.
[46] Lee, *Daniel Defoe*, II, p. 500.
[47] Lee, *Daniel Defoe*, II, p. 351.
[48] *Mercurius Politicus* of August 1718, p. 445.
[49] *An Argument Proving that the Design of Employing and Enobling Foreigners, Is a Treasonable Conspiracy against the Constitution* (London, 1717), p. 51.
[50] *The Family Instructor* (Newcastle-upon-Tyne, 1715), pp. 23-24: Defoe's references to St. Paul are to *Romans* VII, 1 and 18.
[51] *A Collection of Miscellany Letters, Selected out of Mist's Weekly Journal. The First Volume* (London, 1722), p. 192.
[52] *Ibid*, p. 194.
[53] *The Compleat English Gentleman*, ed. Karl D. Bulbring (London, 1890), pp. 111-12.
[54] *Mere Nature Delineated* (London, 1726), pp. 5, 44, 54 and 61.
[55] See Novak, *Defoe And The Nature Of Man*, pp. 39-40 and 42-43.
[56] *An Attempt towards a Coalition of English Protestants* (London, 1715), pp. 8 and 36.

NOTES TO CHAPTER TWO

[1] *Conjugal Lewdness*, pp. 88 and 229.
[2] *Jure Divino. A Satyr* (London, 1706), Bk IV, p. 23.
[3] *Jure Divino*, Bk VIII, p. 4.
[4] For this and the following points see *Review* III, p. 429.
[5] *Jure Divino*, Bk III, p. 26; Bk I, p. 19; Bk II, pp. 4-5; Bk II, p. 10; Bk II, p. 10; Bk IV, p.27; Bk II, p. 10; Bk II, p. 12; Bk IV, p. 27 for Defoe's references to Grotius, Pufendorf, Harrington, Sidney, Locke, and Filmer respectively.
[8] *The Wickedness of a Disregard to Oaths*, pp. 4-5, 7, 9-11, 26-28 and 32.
[9] The section on the blessedness of spiritual peace in *A Hymn to Peace* (London, 1706), pp. 11-14, appears in *Serious Reflections*, pp. 74-75. The lapse

of fourteen years between publication dates shows the self-consciousness with which he cites himself.

[10] *A Speech Without Doors* (London, 1710), p. 5.

[11] See Novak, *Defoe And The Nature Of Man*, p. 69, for the claim that *Serious Reflections* contains Defoe's most systematic discussion of natural law and necessity.

[12] *Serious Reflections*, pp. 26, 21, 23 and 36.

[13] *Ibid*, p. 38. Here Defoe refers to *Proverbs* VI, 30.

[14] *Ibid*, pp. 43-44. Here Defoe adapts *Matthew* XII, 1-8.

[15] *Ibid*, pp. 45 and 59.

[16] *Ibid*, pp. 24 and 37.

[17] See Novak, *Defoe And The Nature Of Man*, p. 2, for a different view.

NOTES TO CHAPTER THREE

[1] *The Present State of the Parties in Great Britain* (London, 1712), pp. 3-4.

[2] Lee, *Daniel Defoe*, III, p. 469.

[3] *Review* IV, p. 453.

[4] *Serious Reflections*, p. 81.

[5] *The Englishman's Choice, and True Interest* (London, 1694), p. 14.

[6] *Reflections upon the Late Great Revolution* (London, 1689), pp. 1-2.

[7] *Ibid*, pp. 36-37 and 40. It is interesting to consider that, while he refuses to regard the political constitution as a religious covenant, Defoe should justify it according to theological analogies. This reflects his desire to accommodate religious and social responsibilities.

[8] *Ibid*, p. 48.

[9] *Ibid*, p. 68. Defoe refers to *Isaiah* XLIX, 8 and II *Corinthians* VI, 1-3.

[10] *An Argument Shewing, That a Standing Army, With Consent of Parliament, Is not Inconsistent with a Free Government* (London, 1698), p. 13.

[11] *The Interests of the Several Princes and States of Europe Consider'd* (London, 1698), p. 13.

[12] *The Two Great Questions Further Considered* (London, 1700), pp. 6-8.

[13] *The Danger of the Protestant Religion Consider'd* (London, 1701), p. [A2].

[14] *Ibid*, pp. 16 and 18.

[15] *Ibid*, p. 19. Defoe refers to *Matthew* XXV, 35-46.

[16] *Ibid*, p. 31. Defoe refers to *Revelation* III, 16.

[17] *Lex Talionis* (London, 1698), p. 7.

[18] John Robert Moore, *Daniel Defoe: Citizen of the Modern World* (Chicago, 1958), pp. 56-57, accounts for the revolutionary nature of this tract. Lee, *Daniel Defoe*, I, pp. 49-50, judges this tract too much in the light of

the failure to prompt an enquiry into Monmouth's legitimacy. He does not mention Defoe's commitment to Monmouth's cause and his criticisms of the aging Anne.

[19] *The History of the Kentish Petition* in *Later Stuart Tracts*, ed. George A. Aitken (London, 1903), p. 172.

[20] *Ye True-Born Englishmen Proceed* (London, 1701), verse 34.

[21] *Legion's Memorial* in *Later Stuart Tracts*, pp. 183-84.

[22] See *Moll Flanders*, pp. 63-65 and 366-68 for further evidence of Defoe's desire to urge stricter legislation against these sanctuaries.

[23] *Selected Poetry and Prose of Daniel Defoe*, ed. Michael F. Shugrue (New York, 1968), pp. 49-50. Citations of *The Mock-Mourners* are also taken from this edition.

NOTES TO CHAPTER FOUR

[1] *An Essay upon Projects*, pp. 243-44.

[2] See Michael Shinagel, *Daniel Defoe and Middle-Class Gentility* (Cambridge, Mass., 1968), pp. 31-32 and 93; Novak, *Defoe And The Nature Of Man*, pp. 18, 28-29, and 154-57; and John McVeagh, "Rochester and Defoe: A Study in Influence," *Studies in English Literature 1500-1900*, XIV (1974), 327-41.

[3] *Review* V, p. 82 and Lee, *Daniel Defoe*, II, p. 346.

[4] Lee, *Daniel Defoe*, III, p. 267.

[5] See *Serious Reflections*: 'My Lord *Rochester*, who was arriv'd to an extraordinary Pitch in this Infernal Learning, acknowledg'd it on his Death-Bed' (p. 91). Rochester is also one of those who 'turn'd all Matters of Faith into Ridicule, burlesqu'd upon Religion it self, and made Ballads and Songs on the Bible' (p. 92).

[6] *Review* IX, p. 116.

[7] *An Essay on the History and Reality of Apparitions* (London, 1727), pp. 308-09.

[8] *Reformation of Manners* (London, 1702), pp. 58-59.

[9] *Review* III, p. 415.

[10] Sutherland, *Daniel Defoe: A Critical Study*, says that Rochester was 'a poet to whom [Defoe] was nearly always ready to grant a special kind of indulgence for the sake of his wit' (p. 110). Usually, however, Defoe's concession of wit to Rochester serves a rhetorical purpose. Defoe's attitude is reflected in this comment in *A Vindication of the Press* (London, 1718), p. 13: 'The only Objection that I do not take upon me to Defend, is, that against Lewd and obscene Poetry in general; (for sometimes the very great Wit may make it excusable) which in my Opinion will admit of but a slender Apology in its Defence.' Defoe is indulgent to Rochester occasionally rather than habitually.

[11] Lee, *Daniel Defoe*, II, p. 31.

[12] *The Political History of the Devil*, p. 530: here Defoe attributes the wit of normally stupid aristocrats to the agency of the devil. Charmed by him, such people can 'reason against all Religion, as strongly as a Philosopher; blaspheme with such a keenness of Wit, and satyrise God and Eternity, with such a Brightness of Fancy, as if the Soul of a *Rochester* or a *Hobbs* was transmigrated into them.'

[13] Compare with McVeagh's view in "Rochester and Defoe" that the references to the poet demonstrate Defoe's inability to be eclectic.

[14] See 'The Fall' in *The Complete Poems of John Wilmot, Earl of Rochester*, ed. David M. Vieth (New Haven, 1968), p. 86.

[15] Lee, *Daniel Defoe*, III, p. 297.

[16] See *The Complete Poems of John Wilmot*, p. 110, ll. 185-86.

[17] Lee, *Daniel Defoe*, II, p. 146.

[18] *Review* IV, p. 395.

[19] Lee, *Daniel Defoe*, III, p. 290 and *A System of Magick*, p. 339.

[20] *An Essay on the History and Reality of Apparitions*, p. 5.

[21] *Review* VIII, p. 846 and *The Complete Poems of John Wilmot*, p. 126, l. 124.

[22] *Review* I, p. 414 and *Mercator: or, Commerce Retrieved*, no. 82.

[23] *Review* VIII, p. 367. See also *Some Account of the Two Nights Court at Greenwich* (London, 1716), p. 62, for more evidence of Defoe's reliance upon Rochester as regards stance: 'My Lord *Rochester* evidently proves there is a Necessity to deal with such Men in their own Way, and to fight them at their own Weapons.'

[24] See *Serious Reflections*, p. 93:
> If it should so fall out, as who can tell
> But there may be a GOD, a *Heaven* and *Hell*?
> Mankind had best consider well, for fear
> 'T should be too late when their mistakes appear.

[25] *A System of Magick*, p. 88.

[26] *The Political History of the Devil*, pp. 300 and 315. Whereas Defoe cites *Matthew* IV, 24 as the source of Christ's encounter with Legion, the actual source is *Mark* V, 9.

[27] *Moll Flanders*, p. 60 and Starr's note, p. 365.

[28] *Robinson Crusoe*, pp. 241, 243, 246, 255, 267, 268 and 275.

NOTES TO CHAPTER FIVE

[1] Lee, *Daniel Defoe*, III, pp. 466-69.

[2] See Maximillian E. Novak, "Defoe's Theory of Fiction," *Studies in Philology*, LXI (1964), 650-68, for an account of Defoe's attitudes to writing which also explains the gap between his theory and his practice.

[3] See *A Vindication of the Press*, pp. 5-7, 11-12, 15, 18 and 27-33.

⁴ Opposite views about Defoe's stance are expressed by Diana Spearman, *The Novel and Society* (London, 1966), pp. 158 and 169.
⁵ *A Collection of Miscellany Letters. The Fourth Volume*, pp. 130-31.
⁶ For the opposite view which claims that eighteenth-century novelists' largest contribution was the blending of romance and realism see Spearman, *The Novel and Society*, p. 113.
⁷ *A General History of the Pyrates*, ed. Manuel Schonhorn (Carbondale, 1972), p. 667.
⁸ *A General History*, ed. Schonhorn, p. 670.
⁹ See Novak, "Defoe's Theory of Fiction," p. 664. John J. Richetti, *Popular Fiction Before Richardson 1700-1739* (Oxford, 1969), pp. 72-73, suggests that Defoe presents the pirates more uniformly than he does.
¹⁰ Although both works are cited in Moore, *A Checklist*, the first is usually thought to be Defoe's and the second not. However, internal evidence of Defoe's authorship of the second is strong.
¹¹ *A Collection of Miscellany Letters. The Fourth Volume*, p. 125.
¹² Lee, *Daniel Defoe*, II, p. 131. This is an adaptation of the fifth line of George Herbert's 'The Church-porch': 'A verse may find him, who a sermon flies.'
¹³ The narrator of *Street-Robberies Consider'd* becomes literate on pp. 9 and 22 whereas Jack reports learning to read and write [*Colonel Jack*, ed. Samuel Holt Monk (London, 1965)] on pp. 7 and 80.
¹⁴ See George Macauley Trevelyan, *The Peace and the Protestant Succession* (London, 1934), pp. 113-14, 271 and 303.
¹⁵ See Justin McCarthy, *The Reign of Queen Anne* (London, 1902), I, pp. 144-63 for an account of Peterborough which accords with Defoe's views.
¹⁶ *Memoirs Of A Cavalier*, ed. James T. Boulton (London, 1972), p. 2.
¹⁷ Compare the argument of the last paragraph with the following: Spearman, *The Novel and Society*, claims that the Revolution had no impact on Defoe's writing (p. 215) and that there is little connection between his narratives and society (p. 248); Richetti, *Popular Fiction Before Richardson*, defines narrative as escapist (p. 5) and maintains that extended narratives become fictions during consumption (p. 7); Sutherland, *Daniel Defoe: A Critical Study*, insists on the split between artist and moralist in Defoe (p. 220); Frederick F. Karl, *A Reader's Guide to the development of the English novel in the Eighteenth Century* (London, 1974), pp. 5-10, maintains that narrative is inevitably counterproductive and subversive and that it detaches the reader from his normal social context. My ideas on Defoe's concept of the writer's role are drawn from *The Storm*, pp. A2-A4, *Conjugal Lewdness*, pp. 17-19, and *An Essay on the Regulation of the Press* (London, 1704), pp. 1-14.

www.ingramcontent.com/pod-product-compliance
Lightning Source LLC
Chambersburg PA
CBHW060333050426
42449CB00011B/2747